LAKELAND YESTERDAY

VOLUME I

For Charles and Cynthia, Holly and Rose
in exchange for many happy hours.

~

And for Bill, who made this book possible.

LAKELAND YESTERDAY
VOLUME I

Irvine Hunt

Smith
Settle

First published in 2002 by
Smith Settle Ltd
Ilkley Road
Otley
West Yorkshire
LS21 3JP

ISBN Paperback 1 85825 168 0
ISBN Hardback 1 85825 169 9

Set in Monotype Bembo

Designed, printed and bound by
SMITH SETTLE
Ilkley Road, Otley, West Yorkshire LS21 3JP

Contents

Acknowledgements

To THE MANY WHO have helped – thank you. They include friends, and those who have become friends, sometimes chance acquaintances, often with good tales, often interested in history, sometimes a little surprised that anyone would be interested in their own stories, and all generous, as these pages show. To them all I offer my thanks.

Especially to author, lecturer and Lakeland enthusiast William Rollinson, a much loved Cumbrian who is greatly missed by so many of us. Thanks to Bill, a knock at the door introduced the publishers of this book, Smith Settle, who from the start said they would like to produce an engaging book. Two, in fact, when only one had been hoped for.

Many generous people have given permission to use pictures and many of their names appear below, though not all for some prefer to remain anonymous. A few, too, are no longer with us, but I wish to acknowledge their help for their families' sakes. A number of the pictures are from family albums and have not been in book form before. A few I have used in my two previous books, *The Lakeland Pedlar* and *Fenty's Album*, both out of print, but the pictures are used again here because many have requested it, and they seemed too good not to repeat. While most of the pictures are at the core of Lakeland, the span at times is wider than that, embracing other parts of Cumbria.

I wish to pay tribute in particular to Harry and Doreen Knipe for endless encouragement, use of photographs, and even 'Never Absent Never Late' medals, as well as many cups of tea down the years; photographer Brian Wade and Sue who have put up with my awful demands to re-photograph old pictures for use here, and always have succeeded and given more help than anyone deserves; likewise Keith Wilkinson who seems able to rescue a picture out of faded yellowness when success seems impossible. My thanks, too, to Stephen White, Cumbria Libraries local history librarian in Carlisle, whose advice and support have been considerable and greatly appreciated. That too could be said of many in the library service of Cumbria, and especially of Christine Strickland, for years the mainstay of Kendal local history library, and now retired; likewise Ron Smith of Barrow-in-Furness Library, also retired, who once let me live for a couple of days in the library safe to look at photographs; my thanks also to Trevor Jones, Workington librarian and writer.

Any mistakes in the text are my own. There would have been a number but for the kindness of several experts, and especially that of David Hay whose wise professional editing judgement came to my rescue. He gave much of his own time to read this ms, and generously bequeathed a mass of corrections, which I have incorporated. Much wise help, too, from Kathleen and Margaret Ashbridge of Caldbeck, and from Nancy Tweddle and the Little family who have done their best to keep the furrows straight.

The others who deserve our thanks are the photographers themselves. The Abrahams, Herbert Bell, Frank Herbert and Mary Fair immediately come to mind, but there are many many more, mostly of a century ago, often unknown. The hope has always been that every picture tells a story, and here a little of their work lives on.

The list of helpers is long. In particular, special thanks for the loan, or supply, and permission to use photographs are due to Geoffrey Perry Abraham, Sue Allen, Jack Allonby, Norman Allonby, Peter Anderson, Eric Arnison, Bessie Askew, John Askew, J F Barker, Colin Barr, Irene Barton, Ross and Josie Baxter, Annie Benn, Margaret Bell, Winifred Blackadder, Norman and Dorothy Blaylock, Sir Christian Bonington, Jim Brown, the Burrow family, Jennifer Butterworth, Dorothy Chalk, The Clark Family, W Clarke, Malcolm and Colleen, Maureen Collins, Stephen Cove, Jimmy Craghill, Anne Croasdale, Cumbria's libraries, in particular Barrow-in-Furness, Carlisle, Grange-Over-Sands, Kendal, Kirkby Stephen, Millom, Penrith, Silloth, Whitehaven and Workington; Adrian Dalton, Phillis Dawson, Derek, Ann Dick, curator, Whitehaven Records Office; Muriel Dover, John William Dover, Drigg and Carleton Parish Council, Joan Day, Eddie Dykes, Beatrice Earl, Richard and Kath Earl, Charlie Ellwood, English Nature: Maggie Robinson and Jacqui Ogden, Kendal; Frank Mawby, Kirkbride; Steve Edge, Peterborough; Evelyn Geddling, Bill Gibson, Gill Greenhalgh, Bill Guest, the Hadwin family, Joe Harper, R R Harrison, John Hurst, Ethel Heathcote, Frank and Louis Herbert, the Herbert family, Jean and John Higgins, Hodge Close Green Slate Quarry, Dr P Honeyman, Tony Ingram, Rev Joe Isaacs, Jimmy Jackson, John Jameson, Geoff Johnson, Windermere Lake Cruises; Suzanne Johnston, Gordon Larkin, W C Lawrie, Tommy Little, the Lomas family, A Mann, Jack Manning, Robin Martakies, St Martin's College (Charlotte Mason), Ambleside; Stephen Matthews, the Bookcase, Carlisle; Margaret Matthewson, the Mayson Family, George Mayson, Nils Minor, Anne Moffat, the Moss family, Bill Mossop, Caroline Mustill, John Nettleton, the Oldfield family, Frank and Kate Pearce, historian Denis Perriam; Geoffrey Perry Abraham, Pauline, Eddie Pool, R Quine, Anne Ramsbottom, Annan Historic Centre; Frank Reynolds, Don Richards, Bluebell Books, Penrith; Maureen Richardson, Archie Ritson, Cedric Robinson, J Saul, David Frank Scott, Diana Scott, Mary Shepherd, Colin Smith, May Smith, South Tynedale Railway Preservation Society, Ronnie Stobart, Meriel Stokoe, collections officer, the Beacon, Whitehaven; Robert Strike, R N Taylor, the Threlkeld family, Ronnie and Joyce Tiffin, George Tinker, Anne Trembath, B Tyson, Robt W A Watson, Isobel White, George Whitley, A Whittaker and N Wilson.

Irvine Hunt
Hutton Roof, 2002

The Good Old, Bad Old Days

H E WAS AN old man, well into his nineties with an astute face, a quiet Cumbrian, and he was looking out onto the farmyard and up towards the fells.

'You know, when I think about it', he said, 'life today is nothing like the life I knew when I was a lad — I mean, the world has changed beyond all belief.'

He couldn't easily have drawn up a list but he meant, for one thing, that you could settle a deal in the old days by a shake of the hand, and few thought of

Ready to set off from the Old Ferry Hotel is the Windermere ferry, still propelled by oars or giant sweeps. The horse has been unhitched from its load to give the ferrymen space to row across the lake, at this point in its middle reach some 560 yards (510m) wide. It was a slow, often hard job, with the weight of centuries in every stroke. The ferry is some 500 years old and a traditional link between Hawkshead on the Lancashire side and Kendal on the Westmorland. Man-powered ferries lasted until 1870 when a steam vessel was launched. Here, though, all appears tranquil and the coming onslaught unsuspected.

A confidential word. Under a shady tree, two friends talk, the one in spiked helmet,
Kaiser Wilhelm II, emperor of Germany, and the other, Hugh Lowther, fifth earl of Lonsdale.
They were photographed during the Germany Army manoeuvres in northern Germany in 1904.
(See page 110.)

In apron and clogs, a young girl is hired at Carlisle Cross. The mistress is handing over a token earl's shilling and a week hence the girl will begin work, probably at a farmhouse where she will stay for six months until the next hiring. She seems little more than thirteen and, though the photographer may have re-staged the picture, there is no mistaking the girl's unhappiness. Youngsters were often accompanied by their mothers or an older sister who would speak up and ensure that the employer seemed a reasonable person. Frequently it was a gamble. Where families were large with perhaps ten or more children, boys and girls of only twelve years were sometimes hired out for no pay at all, to get them out of the house. 'For their eats' — that was the phrase.

breaking the trust it signified. And while many were literate, there were also some around who still signed their name with a cross and were no less worthy for it; that life was at a slower pace; that perhaps there was more common sense about, and perhaps more trust.

'We never locked our doors, didn't even think of it, not till just a few years ago.'

Whatever we have gained in the twentieth century — and it is much — it seems at times that we have lost out, too, a certain quality, perhaps a stronger sense of integrity … when a handshake had the power of a contract.

So this book is about those times, the good old days, the bad old days, for then as now they were a mixture of both, and our children in years to come will

Beatrix Potter and Lady Leconfield at a Lakeland sheep show. The author's hands are clasped,
yet it is her eyes that reveal the most — shrewd and intent. Lakeland people remember this
remarkable woman — writer, artist, naturalist, diarist and farmer — with real affection.
She built herself into farming life so that at times she became indistinguishable from the locals,
leaving her mark on the countryside in a practical and businesslike way.

(See pages 89–96)

The Old Man of the Sea — so they said when they spoke of James Bryson. For more than eighty years he fished the Solway Estuary, living in a dimly lit cottage in the hamlet of Glasson. He first fished, he used to tell, as a lad in petticoats, and after that he never stopped. His white beard and white hair made him a romantic figure, though his life was often harsh enough. Jim Bryson had some good fish hauls. Like most of the fishermen around him, he used stake nets until one day, unexpectedly, to the scorn of other fishermen he decided to fish from a boat. Their attitude changed when they began to see the size of his hauls. He once caught fifty-three grilse and salmon on one tide. On another occasion, with his father, he caught seventy-two salmon, again on one tide. Jim lived until 1940 to the age of ninety-six.

How better to go on a day trip over Lakeland's mountain passes than in a smart open motor car?
This was the way over Buttermere Hause when the road was *'nobbut pinnel and stane'*,
just boulder clay and stone.

likely talk about our time in a similar way. At the core are the people who lived in Cumberland, Westmorland and North Lancashire, or Cumbria as it is now called, embracing the English Lake District. Most of the pictures were taken about the turn of the nineteenth century, though earlier or later ones have been included where it seemed appropriate. Implicit in many of them is something of the quality of life in those times and, wherever possible, the text and the pictures do try to tell a story. A number of first-hand accounts appear here, too. Set in italics, they reveal an element of poignancy which I personally find very engaging.

So many changes. In 1900, scarcely any electricity, or farms with tapped water. Few cars were in Lakeland, though thousands of horses were at work on the land, thousands more on the roads; and thousands of men and women were in service, hired each Whitsuntide and Martinmas at street markets, the oldest labour exchange in the world. Truly a different way of life.

The old society had been changing for a long time, a process that seems to have speeded up in the spell leading up to the First World War, with new farming methods developing, and, significantly, the coming of those motor vehicles which had the power to uproot families by ending — some say destroying — their attachment to place.

And the changes have continued down all the years. Electrification, more mechanisation, the increased use of chemical fertilisers, weedkillers, BSE, bigger farms and ranching, the immense growth of tourism, GM foods, the catastrophe of foot and mouth, and, sometimes less obvious yet taking place, family after family quitting the land after generations of toil.

Beyond all belief, said my old friend. Here, though, is what I hope will prove to be a good dip into the old days, however they may have been.

When Families Were Large

'WASTE NOT, WANT NOT.' The phrase has sounded throughout much of our lives, and it was certainly the outlook of many families in the Lake counties at the start of the last century.

Families were often large with six, eight, or ten children, and sometimes even more. The famous huntsman John Peel of Caldbeck was one of a family of thirteen, and his own family comprised of thirteen.

Traditionally the older children looked after the younger ones; clothes of necessity were passed down, much as now, and it was small wonder if the parents of those large struggling families appeared to age more rapidly than parents of today. Victorian and Edwardian working men of forty often looked sixty or more in old photographs. Pensions were not available for many retired people till 1908. There was no legal retirement age, but you had to be seventy or over to receive a state pension. Many went on working till infirmity stopped them.

Child mortality was high. A faded sepia print passed to me by a friend showed eleven children outside their small cottage in deepest Lakeland. But it revealed only part of the story, for it could not tell of the two children who had died at birth, and it gave no clue to the fate of two more in the picture who were to die before they were eleven, one of TB and one of 'the fever'. The last phrase occurs all too frequently.

Mothers had a hard task feeding and clothing their broods. Yet the best of them were highly capable managers. They cooked on cast-iron ranges the like of which would probably appal many of today's young housewives, with the oven or ovens on one side, and a hot water tank on the other. The brass tap to the water tank was often the brightest polished object in the home. Romantic sounding, but in reality a constant effort was needed to keep the tank filled and so maintain the hot water supply, as well as load the range with sticks and coals. Most of the hot water came from that tank, but some also from the kettle, forever over the fire; or on Monday washdays, from the set pot in the washhouse.

Marathon baking sessions took place, perhaps once or twice a week. Wives made their own bread, cakes, pastries and biscuits, as well as oatcake, oatmeal porridge and skim milk cheese, in some areas called *wangy cheese*, meaning tough. Numerous farmhouses had a backstone on which *haver bread* was made.

A backstone was about the height of a table, usually in a corner of the building with the flu going into the main chimney. Some women travelled from farm to farm and were employed to bake haver bread in loads, and then it was stored in the driest cupboard and used sparingly.

In Lakeland towns, matters were somewhat easier. Numerous small bake-houses once existed. In Kendal, Penrith and Ulverston, for example, they did good business. Housewives mixed the bread at home and when their children went to school they took a batch to the bakehouse. Just anything that was cookable went, a stew, a chicken, a piece of meat. For a few coppers it would be cooked or baked, and the children carried it home steaming hot once lessons were over.

At many an isolated farm, winter supplies often depended on preserving skills. Stewed fruit when cold was covered in clean melted fat which, once hard, was said to make a good airtight seal. Mutton was salted; or smoked. Geese, too, were salted. There was considerable pickling, and wine and syrup making using burnet and rhubarb were popular.

Family life was often hard and few thought it might be otherwise. Sam Hoggarth, whose life as a blacksmith appears on pages 64–66, had five sisters and five brothers. At times they experienced hardship and hunger. During the Great Freeze of 1894-5 his father, a drystone waller, was out of work for seventeen weeks — and thirteen mouths to feed. Many people in that hard time ended in the workhouse penniless. In desperation, Sam's mother and her grandmother took in washing at their cottage in Sawrey, and Sam and a sister collected the dirty clothing from the wealthier houses, carting it home in a wheelbarrow. The children were given the job of carrying in buckets of water while the women got on with the task. The pay was a pittance but that was all they could find to do. Sam said: 'I asked my father: "Father, how ever did you manage?" And his answer has stayed with me all me life. "Nay, I don't know, lad. 'Appen God knows, but I don't".'

A Lakeland small-farm family. Thomas and Elizabeth Lomas and their ten children and dog Nell lived at Middle Dale Park in the Rusland Valley. If they seem somewhat austere-faced, perhaps it was because the act of being photographed was regarded as a solemn occasion for remote country folk. Thomas was a disciplined farmer and strict. His children had to do as they were told and none dared disobey. After this picture was taken, Elizabeth had three more children, thirteen in all, but the last one, Joseph, died as a baby. The eight boys and four girls all grew to adulthood, the boys working mainly in wagoning for Martindale's farm nearby and for Croasdale's woodyard down-valley at Greenodd. The girls worked on the farm. All of the children's faces show signs of having had rickets. From the left, Jim, Tyson, Thomas, Septimus, Margaret, Tommy, Reuben, Jack behind mother Elizabeth, toddler Sarah-Ann, Elizabeth and Ted, who moved as the picture was taken.

All the Pattinsons in the world are said to have originated from the Pattinsons of Patterdale. Whether true or not, one of the best known among them was Lancelot Pattinson, seen here in old age. He was born in 1769 and lived until 1865 when he was ninety-six. As a widower, he dwelt in a shelter in a dark, smoke-filled cave near Goldrill Bridge. The cave became known as Lanty's Castle and to this day there is a Lanty Hill nearby.

The heart of the farmhouse. A cast-iron cooking range at Wath Farm, Caldbeck, about 1900. A fine array of pewterware stands on the shelves above the desk, and the last sheaf of the summer corn hangs from the beam. At ranges like these, meals for six, eight, even ten members of the family and the hired hands were cooked. The Wath kitchen is a much lived-in place: a couple of dried hams; a gun over the range; hazel and oak swill baskets for carrying the washing, the potatoes, coal or firewood. The giant kettle, handy enough for the farmhands to boil a rapidly placed egg or two when the missis wasn't looking, can be raised or lowered on its *rattencrook*, suspended from a crane. Extra well stoked in winter, the range and its stone surround grew comfortably hot, not unlike a radiator. On dark nights the family and, in some farmsteads, the hired hands would gather round the fire and, illuminated by candles or paraffin lamps, would get on with patchwork or quilting, make *proddy rugs* from rag strips, knit socks and stockings, make shirts (no-one ever thought of buying them) or just sit spinning and telling yarns. A century ago the James family farmed at Wath, and today their descendants still do.

Opposite:
This range in a Rusland Valley cottage has the fire at ground level. Smoothing irons stand on the oven and tea caddies line the mantleshelf. On the right, a vital fire lighting aid, a pair of bellows. Primitive though the range appears, they were once quite common in Lakeland. In better-off farmhouses they extended into considerable sophistication, with extra ovens and larger hot water tanks.

It looks romantic, but it was hard work. Many cottages had to rely on village pumps like this in Caldbeck. Water was sometimes carried in yoked buckets, with Monday wash-days the hardest going.

Going modern a century ago. They seemed to weigh a ton, but cookers like this with their ornamental touches were the in-thing if you had a handy gas supply. A pint of water boiled in a mere six minutes. Who could resist it!

Coke, too, for sale. My grandfather remembered when the gas works *gave* coke away for nothing. He wheeled an empty pram to the works and got many a free load, but it all changed as others caught on, and eventually a pram of coke cost sixpence. 'Things are getting worse', he said.

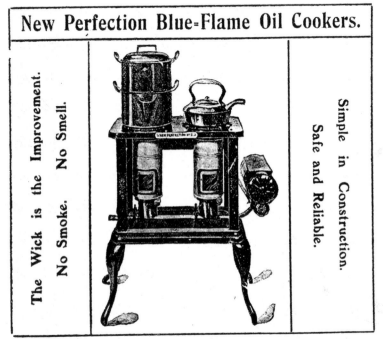
'No smoke. No Smell. Blue-Flame Oil Cookers'. And no need to rely on a gas supply or having to cook over the fire. 'The Wick is the Improvement' claimed this advertisement from the *Furness Year Book* for 1908.

Oil cookers sounded ideal for Lakeland's remote farms and cottages, and though many used this kind of stove to good purpose, the claims were sometimes over-ambitious. At the rural school which I attended as a five year old, our paraffin stove never did achieve perfection. At day-end the pupils whiffed of paraffin and some of us were fated to have all too many baths.

Opposite:

In shawl and hat, a matronly Lakeland housewife stands at her *dolly tub* in Ambleside. Around her are a dolly stick on legs, used to pound the clothes, a metal lifter and, behind, the result of hard work, an array of clean clothes.

Depending on the household, this weekly task often entailed a long getting-ready session. An ample pile of sticks had to be gathered in to fuel the cast-iron *set pot* in the washhouse, usually a Saturday job, and it was up early on Monday morning to light the fire and heat the water.

Clothes were washed in the big tub, scrubbed in the smaller rubbing tub, using a ribbed zinc rubbing board, and then rinsed in hot water, bailed in by the lifter. Usually the whites and towels were boiled in the set pot, built in at about table height. Dolly blue was used to improve the whiteness, and the clean clothes were fed through a hand-turned mangle with wooden rollers, which could devour pearl buttons whole-sale. Later, taped buttons were introduced which did not break so easily.

Usually the washing was hung on lines, though some women preferred to spread the clothes to dry on thorn hedges. Bleaching the whites by the sun was regarded as a good practice. Spreading them on the grass was also said to help with the bleaching process.

Mangles similar to the one in this billhead were common enough objects in washhouses and backyards. Usually made of cast-iron, they worked efficiently until the wooden rollers wore in the middle and needed replacing. As recent as the 1980s a friend and I found an old warehouse in Penrith, its shelves loaded with dozens of new mangle rollers. All were in perfect condition, still in their original wrapping papers, thick in dust, awaiting customers. Bedsteads, as shown on the bill, were in widespread use in Lakeland. Bits still turn up today blocking gaps in hedges.

This heavily carved cupboard above is a brideswain and is seen at Lane Head, Patterdale.

Brideswains were sometimes made to celebrate a marriage, perhaps as a wedding gift, and were said to have been carried in the marriage procession on a *wain* or wagon to the couple's new home. They are also known as press cupboards and court cupboards. They were found in many seventeenth- and eighteenth-century yeoman farmhouses, with two early versions, at Common Farm, Windermere, and High Wray Farm, being dated 1628. Others still exist. Often they were built into wooden stud partitions, as here, and were complete pieces of furniture with backs and sides. The generally accepted use, cited by William Rollinson in his book *Life & Tradition in the Lake District,* is that they were bread cupboards, used to store *haver* or *clap bread*. This was made from oatmeal and so called because it was clapped between the hands to flatten it during making. Versions of this bread are still eaten in Norway.

This brideswain is carved with the date 1660 and the initials L H I, for Lancelot and Isabel Harrison.

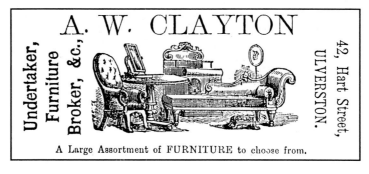

A spinner at work. Spinning wheels were found in many a Lakeland kitchen, both for home use as well as for cottage industries and the chance to earn a little extra cash.

Opulence and all the security of comfortable clutter. The drawing room at Ellerthwaite, Windermere, with plenty for the servants to dust.

Thomas Moffat, handloom weaver of Wigton, sits within the circle of his family, tightly buttoned and dressed in his Sunday best. It's Thomas's one hundredth birthday celebration in August 1890 and, to commemorate the event, Henry Banks of Highmoor Mansion, Wigton, invited the weaver to his home, where Thomas was wined and dined, and finally photographed by Henry, who was a keen photographer. The result was this fine picture of a Victorian and his family.

John Miles Moss, the parson at St John's Church, Bowness, Windermere, and his daughter Ester fetch a kettle of water from the beck during a picnic on Helvellyn in 1902. Ester and her brothers and sisters spent their childhood at Windermere. She became a nurse during the First World War and later ran a boarding house in Windermere. Her fondest memory was of her father ...

We were a Victorian family. We were brought up in a very big house, which became known as Annisgarth, and in our childhood days was called Helm. It had twenty-six acres [10ha], I think, with paddocks and a huge kitchen garden and perfectly lovely views right across Windermere.

Helm had big back quarters, now houses; we had our own laundry, now another house; we had our own stables and those too have been turned into houses.

At the back there were all sorts of little places. Mother was interested in photography and had a dark room, and we had kennels. One time we had a tweenie maid. She once said: 'Please, sir, the mistress has gone to the dogs.'

The house had no electricity. We had gas mantles, then at Helm on my tenth birthday we got electricity. Our nursery had a switch and we dashed up and turned it on. It was a great treat, better than any present.

We wore lovely clothes. Lovely pinafores. I loved my pinafores. In the winter we used to wear sailor suits, and one year my mother put us into Highland gear. My mother used to experiment with us, me especially as a baby. She found that putting me in the sun made me sneeze. I pulled such funny faces. She put me in the sun deliberately, I think, so that I could make her laugh. She treated me rather like a live doll. She was only twenty when I was born … there was no fuss or bother and I think it was a very good way.

We were brought up very strictly. We might not have had any money at all in the family from the way we were treated. We were never stuffed with sweets and we had to obey on the instant. My little sister once wanted something at dinner, and she said: 'Oh, mother, can't I?' And I said: 'Don't be silly. You know when mother says no she means no.'

Mother used to go her own way and we had to fit in. That was, I think, the secret of Victorians. They weren't questioned. 'We are going on a picnic today.' And that was that. We weren't asked if we'd like to go. My childhood was not very exciting. We were certainly looked after, but never spoiled. We were never considered and I'm glad of it. I think children today have a rough time because they have no training and no crosses to bear. They've just been allowed to go their own way and I think they are suffering for it.

We were a very large family and looking back I think we must have been a very selfish one. We were so engrossed in ourselves that we really didn't bother very much about other people. We had friends who came to stay in the summer, and we spent all the summer either picnicking or playing games. It was really a very selfish life. I wouldn't go back to it for anything, though it was all the luxury in the world. No.

My father — I wish I had expressed my love to him more. He was an odd man out in a way because my mother and sisters clicked so very much that father used to go into his library a great deal.

He was always made to go for a picnic on his birthday. I've got a snapshot of him, which I love dearly. It's one of me as a young woman, on the slopes of Helvellyn on my seventeenth birthday. We were carrying a kettle called a Devon Jenny. Marvellous *because they boiled so quickly. We forced father to take picnics on his birthdays. I was very fond of him. We had a long way to go for water and the picture was of us coming back. Mother adored going on picnics, but we children were so bored sitting still in a crowded wagonette. We were always so thankful when it was to Easedale because it was a shorter drive. When we heard it was to Thirlmere our hearts sank into our boots.*

When the war came in 1914 it released me from home. My father and I were very close and he was upset and it was a really lovely home. But I felt there must be something for me to do, and I never lived at Helm again. I went nursing at Newcastle-on-Tyne. The war I loathed. You couldn't open the papers but you saw that one of your friends or relations had been killed in the trenches. How we dreaded the word. That was the most awful time. I was nursing in Newcastle during the whole of the war. They had extra wards built for the wounded. Some nights we were told: 'Don't go to bed, there's a convoy coming.' Then you'd hear the rumble rumble of wheels and the wounded men would be carried in. One night we were told there were 100 coming, and it was 400. We had no beds. The wounded were lying on the corridors. They arrived still bound with the bandages put on from the trenches in France. They'd come from the war fields, crossed the Channel, they'd had this great long train journey up to Newcastle, and they were the pluckiest and most marvellous, absolutely marvellous brave men. It was very sobering.

When there I saw my first Zeppelin. I was a junior nurse and cooking supper outside, a couple of sausages. 'Oh, Mossy, they said, don't stay outside cooking. Come in!' The sister was so urgent. We stood on the hospital veranda and the Zeppelin came sailing right before us. We thought it was coming straight at the hospital and the sister swore at it. And we saw the bombs dropping. They hit offices and we saw flames. But they did not get us or the factories.

Seen and not Heard

'BE SEEN AND NOT HEARD.' Down the years, how children have groaned at those momentous words. For many they were once the norm. In Victorian times belief in the existing order was deep-seated and implanted in childhood education. In schools, corporal punishment was harsher than in most homes. In Edwardian England the authority of the parents, especially of father as head of the household, was accepted with less question than now. Children were expected to respect their parents, and most did.

Young people in general would expect to leave school at thirteen to fourteen and probably be courting by sixteen, though the average age for marriage was twenty-six.

At the lower end of the scale, there was considerable poverty with much pinching, scraping and want. Infancy especially was a dangerous time and not until the first decade of the twentieth century did infant mortality in towns begin to fall, due in part to improved sanitation, and a vigorous stress on health clinics, germ-free milk and breast feeding.

Throughout the land it was the children of the middle and the upper classes who grew taller, who lived longer. For the Edwardians, life expectancy on average was under fifty years. That was all.

Proud mothers in stylish hats with a host of bonny entrants at a baby show in Millom. Many would definitely be heard as well as seen.

Young Lakelanders paddle in the shallows of the River Leven at Newby Bridge, Windermere. Even here, there's a baby or two to nurse.

All togged up in bonnet and lace collar, little Frank Herbert puts on a brave face despite his girl's clothing. For long enough it was the custom for little boys to be dressed up to look like little girls, and even to have their hair in curls or locks. Young Frank seems to have escaped the locks bit, but suffered the baby tag for a while, though seemingly cheerfully. Most little boys were switched into something more manly like breeches at about four. Frank was kept in skirts until he was six.

When a young man, he worked with his brother Louis in the successful Herbert family photography business opposite St Martin's Church in Bowness, Windermere. Their father, Henry, took this picture. In May 1912 Frank was the first person to take an aerial photograph of Windermere, adventurously leaning out through the lattice-work structure of a waterplane with his half-plate camera as the aircraft flew up the lake at about forty-five miles (70km) an hour.

A babe in the wood … The photographer was French and staying at the Victorian Temperance Hotel in Alston. He was, he told hotelier Emma Gladstone, on a special mission. And this picture of a young woman and the cheerful little baby was the result. It was taken at the Firs, Alston, after Emma had sacrificed her pale mauve wedding dress and cut it up to make the giant mushroom props. She went further, even supplying a meal of fried frogs' legs for the photographer who, after all, was French. The picture is reputed to have gone on to greater things and been used as an advertisement for cameras.

Little Evelyn Geddling poses determinedly in Caldbeck in her Sunday best, 1908. Evelyn's parents kept a shop in the village, and sold everything from treacle out of barrels to flowers in buckets at the door. At its counter, children handed over halfpennies for a treasure from a wooden box, known as Geddling's Dip. Evelyn, who later ran the shop herself, lived all her life in the village, and when she was eighty-five she published her first book, *Geddling's Dip*, her childhood memories of Caldbeck and its people. This picture was its cover. Two further books followed, *Dear Mary* and, in 1997 when she was ninety-seven, *A Second Dip*.

Barefooted and lean, their clothes outgrown these Whitehaven boys, and others like them, had the daily task of carrying buckets of water from the hand pumps down in the town back up to their homes, which often had no taps. Well-splayed toes suggest that neither boy had worn any footwear.

Opposite, top:
Well-to-do and well dressed. The Gaddam children enjoy themselves in the thirty-acre (12ha) grounds of their new home at Brockhole, Windermere. The house was built for a Manchester textile merchant, William Henry Gaddam, who moved in with his family in 1900. William was married to Edith Potter, a cousin of the author Beatrix Potter, and occasionally Beatrix visited them at Brockhole. Today the house, and its garden, which runs down to the edge of Windermere, is the busy Lake District National Park visitor centre.

Opposite, bottom:
Three Edwardian brothers all set on mischief. The Holmes lads (from the left, John, Arthur and William) give a biff of helpful propulsion to their pet donkey in a field at the top of Alston. Their clothes include some hefty clogs and, in the case of John and little Arthur, cape collars to their jackets. William's white collar is washable and at one stage would have been made from celluloid. When worn out, its use could be extended by cutting it up into pieces, rolling tightly in paper and setting it on fire as foul-smelling stink bombs.

Long ago it seems now, there was a time when more than anything else every boy —
and many a daring girl — longed to own a sailor suit. Charlie Ellwood of Oxen Park
in High Furness was one of the lucky ones, and he wore it and wore it and wore it.

Not that Charlie ever went to sea. As a man, he and a brother were farmers,
chopping the kindling late at night, sitting in their chairs by the iron range, shooing
the cats out of the ovens and then baking the bread. Charlie usually was the one who
took the lead. To a few he seemed old fashioned, and perhaps he was a little, for
sometimes he led a cow along the road on a loop of string, and he believed firmly in
many of the old ways, and especially that you should never let anyone down. When
Charlie shook your hand on a deal, it was more binding than any written contract.

Not quite a normal bathing scene in Lakeland. This exception was reported to be near Derwentwater.

The tide is in and the girls take a paddle at the sea's edge at Silloth.

Stick in hand, a boy drover keeps the sheep moving through Whitehaven. Children as young as five sometimes acted as drovers.

Opposite:

Girls on their way to school at High Cunsey, 1908. At one time it seemed that just about every country schoolgirl in Lakeland wore outfits similar to these here: straw hats or berets, the hair long, often in a tress and ribboned, high button boots or clogs, and pinafores over their dresses. Always, it seemed, those pinafores.

The children took their *bait* or lunch with them and one of the normal sights in the schoolroom, especially in winter, was the collection of tin cans standing in a circle round a hot iron stove. The tins of milk or cold tea warmed slowly during the morning's lessons, with teacher's kettle atop. Luckier pupils put eggs in their tins so they might be hard boiled by *bait time*.

From the left there's Florence Bibby, Irene Atkinson, Eleanor Bibby, Hannah Bateson, Hilda Wilkinson, Beatrice Bibby and Gertie Walker. Perhaps there was an egg in the tin carried here by Beatrice.

Cumbrian children were often expected to pull their weight in more ways than schooling. On their way to lessons, many had to drive cattle to the pastures, as well as walk them home again later for milking. In the summer months, at least, children were expected to help deliver milk, butter or eggs round their neighbourhood. A child of nine can often eat as much as a grown person — that was the view. So thrifty families expected them to help with the daily tasks.

Morning exercise at Mungrisdale School. Headmistress Blanche Bott peeps from the doorway as her assistant, Alice Barnfather, puts the pupils through their drill in the flagged yard. The school, at the foot of Ravens Crag, Bowscale Fell, was opened in 1835 and this picture was taken at its centenary. An early church school, it became a private house and a post office.

Lively Blanche was a vicar's daughter, young, intent on teaching and, more than anything, doing it well. Despite some opposition, Blanche was appointed headmistress of Mungrisdale School on the edge of the northern fells. She had taught a little at the school already, but it was still a daunting prospect that first day in the 1920s as she cycled the four and a half miles (7km) from Troutbeck Station to the remote hamlet, for she knew that most of the school managers resented a woman being made a head. After all, a woman could not teach …

At Mungrisdale I was only a supply teacher at first, one pushed in by the education authority. They ruled that one! But I had no help from the managers; they despised women teachers. The second time I was appointed to Mungrisdale, though, I went because I was asked to do so. The managers said that if they had to have a woman they might as well have one they knew, even though I was still only in my twenties. So I got the job, though I'll admit it, that first year was very lonely and depressing and I used to wander alone on the fells above the school seeking some sort of solace in the beauty of the land. It wasn't the only compensation, of course. I like children and despite my doubts I am a determined person.

There was one big classroom, thirty feet by sixteen feet [9m x 5m], with an iron stove for heating and two smelly oil-lamps for lighting. Miss Watson had the young ones, and I had the older ones. There were fifty-eight children, some of them quite big farmers' boys. Soon after I had first arrived, one lunchtime the hefty lads went up on the moss and collected all the barbed wire and such they could and when I returned from dinner they had blocked up a doorway. It was a challenge! Well I don't know how I did it ... I stood them all in a line, about eight or nine of them, some taller than me and, of course, I had a high desk on a platform so I got on that ready for a set-to. Without knowing why, I went down behind the boys and suddenly pulled their legs from under them with my hands, so that they fell to the floor! They looked very foolish ... taken aback, and I told them what I thought of them and ordered them to take all the wire back. And to my relief, they did. But I often wonder how I managed to make them do it, even thirty-three years later, for I was the head for that long.

In winters we were often snowbound. We had to keep the school open even if the snow was two or three feet deep. The children walked in in their clogs and some arrived starved. Once I was going to the school and saw a small pair of clogs sticking out of a drift. Nothing else. Poor Tommy, one of the Wilsons, I think. He had his bag and had fallen into the snow. I grabbed the feet and pulled him out. He was only five years old.

Despite the iron stove, it was not warm in school, but the children wore thick clothes, corduroy. On the bitterest cold mornings the little boys often ate all their lunch by eleven o' clock; by noon they were hungry and often they had mine. They weren't poor. They were farmers' children. But they were hungry.

Teaching toys were non-existent. No bricks. I taught their tables with beer bottle tops, nice and colourful. The children brought them from the Mill Inn and we laid out their tables in bottles tops on the floor. Two times, three times ... we'd hundreds of tops in the end. It produced results, realisations: 'Oh, Miss Bott, we needn't have done all that! We could just have added one at the end in our heads.' It wasn't much, but it was success.

The managers ... they were not all difficult, but they tried to insist that not only had I to keep order inside school, but outside too if anything happened, such as a window being broken at the blacksmith's. Or the boys would stop up the mill race with stones and such. The managers blamed me. Said I ought to punish them. They had a special meeting to discuss it. But Lady Mabel Howard, one of the managers, said I was responsible only during the day and it was ridiculous to insist I be responsible the rest of the time. Well that ended that.

You had to fight for your rights and being a woman made it harder. Another time I was told there was to be a meeting about me, because the children were swearing. Farmers' children! I scotched that one, pointing out that I did not swear and had they never heard a farmer swear — at his sheep, at his dog? No one dared answer me that.

As time passed I became very happy at my work. I lodged at 15s [75p] a week in various cottages. My pay was £120 a year. Somehow in my life I had not moved all that far — I was born at Hayton, one of twelve children; father was vicar there and later at Ousby, and Cotehill, and Newlands. Teaching suited me. So did Mungrisdale. Even the inspectors, looking back, were perhaps not as bad as they first seemed. Well, not so bad ...

One morning I heard the school door open during prayers. We all had our eyes shut and hands together. I thought it was a late pupil. 'Stand there! Put your hands together, and shut your eyes', I ordered. To my horror when I opened my own it was the inspector. He was praying too. He saw the funny side, but the children did not dare laugh. The inspectors were very strict.

At Christmas we had a tree and a party planned for three o'clock. At dinner time the children tied up all their books with string and put them tidily under their desks. Then they ran home to change into party clothes. But at one o'clock in came two inspectors and they said we had to go on with our ordinary lessons. All the books had to be got out and undone again. The inspectors insisted on seeing everything. The children were still in their party clothes as the inspection went on. There was to be no singing till three. It made no difference, the party had to wait.

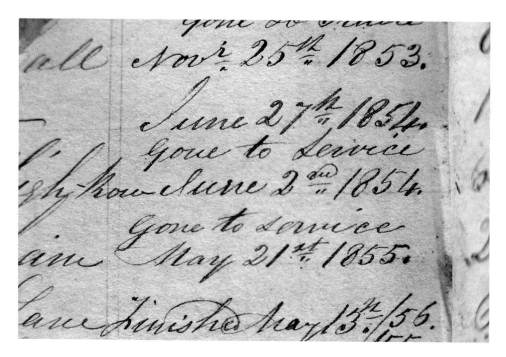

Hutton Roof School log book, Cumberland.

A rural schoolroom at Pennington, Low Furness, 1900. Hinged wooden desks are folded down and heavy cast-iron frames ensure the minimum of desk shift, though few ever did manage to cut out the loud slam of the bench seats. Lines of writing slates stand in slots and the porcelain inkwells are at the ready. A favourite game was to dip a roll of blotting paper in the inkwell and push the blobby wodge into the ear of the child in front. The cane was the normal reward, as well as an occasional wodge in one's own ear. At the far end of the classroom is a cast-iron stove. Pupils tended to roast at that end in the winters, and suffered a slow warming-up at the other, with shivery Mondays worst after the weekend.

Plenty seems to be happening, with pots of plants in all three windows and the walls crowded with pictures — the one bottom left by courtesy of Bovril, always keen to catch its customers young.

Hutton Roof School Log

August, 1912.   Admitted a boy and found that he is unable to talk.

28 April, 1917.   Admitted a new scholar, Thomas Blackley. His mother tells me that owing to living up at the mines and getting the poorest of nourishment he is very delicate and shy.

12 October, 1917.   The girl Doris Dawson, infants, has succumbed to an attack of peritonitis. The children have subscribed for a wreath. This is the first child dying while attending this school.

Charlotte Mason, a remarkable woman who founded a teacher training college in Ambleside and who pioneered education ideas in advance of her time. Born in Bangor in 1842, she was brought up in Liverpool and educated by her parents. Orphaned at the age of sixteen, she entered the first and at the time the only training college for the teaching profession — the Home and Colonial in central London. The future teacher was clear about her aims:

'I knew teaching was the thing to do, and above all, the teaching of poor children.'

But she was intent on much more. After teaching at a girls' school in Worthing, Charlotte at twenty-two wrote: 'I am as soon as possible to have a girls' school of my own.'

Fired with enthusiasm, she took a variety of teaching positions, and also began lecturing to parents and teachers on her approach to education. In Bradford in 1887 her scheme for a society of parents, teacher training and home study was initiated — the Parents' National Educational Union. The PNEU embraced intellectual instruction with physical fitness, moral training and religious loyalties.

By 1864, Charlotte had come to know the Lake District and especially Ambleside. In 1891 she moved to the town and in 1892 her college opened in Springfield House with four students. Two years later, with thirteen students, she moved to Greenbank (Scale How). From that site the college expanded, a considerable task, for she had no capital and had to work to a strict budget.

At the heart of Charlotte's thinking was the belief that education was a process of discovery, that the environment was important, and that great things happen when men and mountains meet. She told her students: 'You have come here to learn — not to teach, but how to *live*.' She saw Ambleside as 'an unwalled university, dedicated to plain living and high thinking'.

The college was founded on the principle that education should be child-centred — at that time a concept regarded by many as quite new. At Ambleside, parents were invited to send their young children daily to the lecture room in the town where students taught them free of charge. Out of this grew the Practising School, Fairfield. The students taught a week at a time and took turns to supervise the boarding house. Each senior student had to give a criticism lesson to the children, observed by the principal, staff and fellow students. It worked well, with the fellow students often proving to be the most critical.

Charlotte was the principal at Ambleside until her death in 1923, after which her name was given to the college, though she would never allow that while she lived. Lancaster University ran Charlotte Mason College for a time and today it is still a lively teacher-training college. Officially it is now St Martins and is administered by St Martins College, Lancaster, as part of their campus, though Charlotte's name is still around and the memory of a remarkable woman lives on.

Trainee teachers put their hearts into outdoor exercise at Charlotte Mason College, Ambleside. The exercises included tossing balls into the air and catching them, as well as vigorous sessions of swinging small pairs of dumbbells.

'Never Absent, Never Late. Jany 1902 – Decr 1904.' Nine proud children at Askam National School, North Lonsdale, show off their blue-ribboned attendance medals.

The lads in knickerbockers, the girls in pinafore dresses, each of them has two medals which were inscribed: 'With All Thy Getting Get Understanding' (see inset). Many schools presented similar tokens to model pupils as a prize for perfect attendance, and even in recent times some schools in Cumbria still gave printed certificates.

Centre, front, is Edwin Knipe of Askam, the youngest of a family of eight children. Edwin began attending the village school when he was four. He walked a mile (1.5km) each way through all weathers and earned four medals. In 1910, aged sixteen, he began an apprentice-ship as a watchmaker and jeweller at Davies's in Barrow-in-Furness, cycling the six miles (9.5km) from home. With three of his brothers, he served in the Westmorland and Cumberland Yeomanry in the Great War and all survived except, ironically, a fifth brother, Walter, a civilian who was killed in an accident at Barrow shipyard. Edwin the skilled watchmaker worked loyally for the same family in the same small workroom for fifty-four years. Rarely absent, rarely late, he retired when he was seventy.

The children line up at Wiggonby School, Wigton, the girls in clean button boots and apron dresses, the boys in caps and boots, hopefully clean. On this occasion, Edith Tiffin, who was a bit of a character, has turned up determined to strike her own brand of individualism and wear her own dark dress, no matter what the teacher says.

Getting to school the hard way. A boy walks the plank amid the ruins of Skelwith Bridge near Ambleside. Fierce floods tore the stonework apart, but there was no missing lessons. The local schoolmaster, keen to ensure that everything continued as usual during rebuilding, at times rowed his pupils across the river himself. The bridge, linking North Lancashire and Westmorland, has been washed down more than once, and though somehow the picture does not appear to be all that old, the damage shown here is thought to date from the floods of the 30th September 1890.

Going to Church

THE CHURCH IN our grandparents' and great-grandparents' time played a more significant role in both spiritual and social life than is the case today.

At Fingland in North Cumberland, when Mary Shepherd was a young woman at her father's farm, going to church was compulsory. Mary was one of six children and their father John demanded obedience. On Sundays, as sexton, he rarely missed attending church, and from time to time after a service he questioned his children, asking if they too had attended. Mary never forgot the occasions when he said he had missed seeing her there, and asked where she had been sitting, who had been in front of her, who behind, who to left and who to the right. Experience taught Mary to be sure she memorised all around her.

In most of England, church attendance had fallen, especially in towns, though almost all children attended Sunday school. In the Cumbrian rural areas the schools were usually well attended. Evelyn Geddling of the little village of Caldbeck, as a child went to the local Wesleyan chapel, especially at the Sunday school anniversary weekend in May. On that occasion a platform in front of the pulpit was extended right across the chapel, and raised seats were put in at the end of the pulpit. All the girls wore new dresses and new ribbons, and the boys were expected to be in new suits. Each child had to recite a text, and was expected to know when to stand up in the correct order to say his or her piece.

Whatever might happen on weekdays, on Sundays dancing was not allowed, nor whistling, nor singing, other than hymns. The strictest families allowed no magazines or newspapers to be read other than perhaps the *Methodist Recorder* and similar publications. Journals such as the popular *John Bull* had to languish under cushions until Monday. Knitting was often forbidden (though sometimes practised secretly under the bed quilt) and swearing was considered outrageous. If hell were allowed a mention in the pulpit, damn at home was unthinkable.

Yet life was not negative. The church was often the social mainstay for many Cumbrians. There were temperance meetings, clothing clubs, rummage sales (to repair the church organ), Band of Hope meetings, popular socials and dances in the local schoolrooms, technical instruction on horticulture, Bible Society meetings, and magic lantern entertainments at which the pictures were 'beautifully manipulated by the Vicar' and were 'well thrown onto the screen' as parish magazines reported.

For entertainment, nothing quite seemed to equal the annual church choir concert in the parish room, which, unless heavy snow fell, invariably took place 'in the presence of a large, enthusiastic and orderly audience among whom were many ladies and gentlemen from a distance'.

Thus, in Rusland Valley, High Furness, where Mrs Gregson played the pianoforte in her usual brilliant style, Miss Postlethwaite rendered capitally *Rock me to Sleep, Mother;* Mr Ballinger, in character, sang *John Peel,* perfectly in tune; and there were numerous dialogues, in particular that by Mr William Wilkinson 'splendidly done, and causing roars of laughter'. A final glee, *Let the Hills Resound* by the entire choir, 'splendidly conducted by Mr Ronald Teasdale, earned hearty cheering and testified how deeply grateful was the audience for such a rich musical treat'.

Outings, likewise, were not to be missed and sometimes were on an amazingly large scale. Sunday school treats from Ulverston early in the last century, usually on Fridays in the summer, went to venues such as Holker Park, Lakeside and Arnside. The railway fare from Ulverston to Cark station for a Holker outing was 3d (1.25p) per child and 5d (2p) for an adult. On these trips as many as 1,000 children travelled, accompanied by 500 adults. Adults had to pay, but the children were paid for and received refreshments free. Quines bakers of Ulverston had the catering franchise, charging 3d for each scholar and 7d for each grown-up. The children received four cakes in a bag and lots of tea in mugs, and they sat on the ground; the adults had ham sandwiches, pies and cakes, and sat at tables. Even these tables, along with wooden forms and a mass of crockery, were transported by a second contractor especially on these occasions, and all were assembled in time for tea, which was served to the strains of the town band playing stirring tunes, including *Onward Christian Soldiers.*

Guests crowd in front of Castle Sowerby's new Methodist chapel at Sour Nook, Sebergham. It's the 5th June 1907, and the official opening day. Made of corrugated iron and lined in pine, it became known affectionately as the Tin Chapel. It could seat more than 100 people comfortably, and was built both as a chapel of workshop and a public hall. On this opening day a giant bazaar was held, and across the road from the chapel a large marquee was erected and great quantities of tea were served.

Traffic was heavy with people coming from afar, mainly by horse-drawn vehicles, but also by motor cars. At Sour Nook, the innkeeper Miss Jackson placed her stables at the disposal of the crowd, as well as opening the inn's large boardroom, where a talk on 'Methodism and the Community' was given by a Mrs Stobbart of Carlisle.

Opposite:

A report of a concert by the Rusland Parish Church choir, from the parish magazine:

'This took place on Friday January 24th [1902], and despite very unfavourable weather, proved a great success. With the exception of one or two front seats, the Parish Room was thoroughly well filled.

The members of the choir dressed in costume as a troupe of "White Coons," gave a variety entertainment consisting of songs, choruses, recitations, jokes, stump speech, &c., in excellent style, as was testified by frequent rounds of applause. When all did so well, it is quite unnecessary to single out any performer for special mention.

The second part of the programme was contributed by friends, and consisted of songs, reading and a humorous sketch entitled a "Happy Pair." For interest and fun, the second part was in nothing behind that contributed by the coons.'

When a Sunday school demonstration took place in Alston, the turnout was often impressive. This was the scene on Whit Monday in 1914.

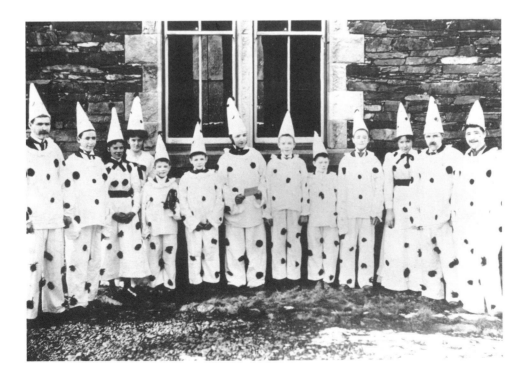

Devout faces, spectacles and the dedicated look of missionary zeal — a section of the crowd at the world-famous Keswick Convention. It was founded in 1875 in a modest tent by Canon Harford-Battersby, the Vicar of St John's, Keswick, and by Robert Wilson of Broughton Grange, near Cockermouth, a member of the Society of Friends. The enthusiasm for the project astonished its founders. Some 200 people took part in the first inter-denominational crusade, and the idea soon grew so that by 1883 a tent for 800 was planned, and even that proved to be too small. The convention has thrived for more than a century. Today it is one of the world's great gatherings of Christians and the slogan is still the one that was suggested by Robert Wilson: 'All One in Christ Jesus.' Not every member of the clergy has viewed its evangelism with total warmth; yet no one who has attended the convention can deny the air of excitement, nor mistake the vigour and fervour of the crowds that flock in from far and wide each summer.

Opposite:
During Keswick's Convention week, there was no mistaking that local booksellers had also caught a little of the religious fervour. Nothing surely could equal the enterprise of Chaplins in Station Street. Hardly a foot of advertising space wasted. Hymns, magazines 'for the deepening of spiritual life', Sankey's sacred songs and solos, as well as a good sprinkling of appropriate authors with 'Rev' before their names, all displayed prominently. Elsewhere in the town, girls walked with sandwich boards advertising religious newspapers, patrolling the roads determined to help sell Christianity in print. In Helvellyn Street and elsewhere, extensive displays of religious books and leaflets were spread out on stalls in front of houses. The convention still takes place each July, but Chaplins bookshop, alas, after trading for more than 100 years, has closed, and another shop has taken its place.

The busy tent in which the Keswick Convention was held at Skiddaw Street. That it became world famous could not be doubted for on one occasion at least, and perhaps on many others, no fewer than twenty different nationalities were represented in the crowded marquee.

These two young men seem ready to take the church abroad in a shiny new Church Missionary Society van, seen in Keswick. It is all set for overseas work, complete with a portable organ, bicycle and an arrow windvane. The CMS was launched in London in 1799, mainly to meet the spiritual needs of the West Africans. But at first no English missionaries could be found, so German Lutherans were employed. This was CMS van number one.

One Guinea Reward.

WHEREAS, some Persons are in the habit of disturbing the Minister and Congregation in *New-street*, during divine Service on Sabbath-evenings, by throwing Stones at the Door, and otherwise improperly conducting themselves, in open violation of the Laws of *God* and their *Country*. Whosoever will give information of the Person or Persons so offending, shall on conviction of the Party, receive the above Reward by applying to

Thomas Bersey, Minister.

Ulverston, December 2d. 1809.

G. ASHBURNER, PRINTER, ULVERSTON.

It's a Man's World

WHILE WORK FOR Edwardian boys and girls began as soon as they left school at fourteen, many at first were in low-paid menial jobs. Apprenticeships for the boys usually came later.

Edwardian Britain was the most urban nation in the world, with a mere seven per cent of the country's work force still in agriculture. Many Cumbrian farmworkers, both men and women, sought jobs through the twice-yearly hirings in the towns, at Whitsuntide and Martinmas (in November), with the chance every six months of moving to another farm if the first spot did not suit.

Cumbrian girls and women, if they did not want to work on farms, and sought a servant's post, turned to agencies in shops, or women's group-meetings in church halls. Others watched the advertisements in local newspapers, or found a place by word of mouth. Servant girls from rural Cumbria were much sought after by townsfolk. Nationally, domestic service was the largest single occupation, with one third of all women as servants. It was cheaper for the middle-class family to employ maids than to buy labour-saving devices, such as vacuum cleaners, which of a kind were available. The working week of fifty-five hours or more dominated life for many. Entries in log books of rural schools again and again show the same three words after a child's name: 'Gone to service'. In the 1891 census for England and Wales, more than 107,000 girls became servants when under the age of fifteen, and this early opportunity of employment contributed to the emptying of rural area of young girls.

For Cumbrian men, manual work included the possibility of slate quarrying, forestry, farming, iron and steel working, ship building, mining and other jobs. Iron ore miners were not all local; some came from the Isle of Man, Wales and Cornwall. Many settled in Ulverston, Askham and Millom. Early in the mornings at Ulverston they walked out of town wearing their battered hats, to work at distant Dalton in Furness. They had a belt or rope round their waist, a tin bottle of tea and a tin box hanging on. They wore clogs and carried a dozen tallow candles which came from the candle factory in Candlehouse Yard. After work, they were covered in dust from the ore; pink faces, pink clothes. Even on a wet day the road back into town was pink from the steady clatter of their clogs.

But not everyone was lucky enough to have a job. Many families were often at the poverty line, and in all this mother bore most of the burden, because the man, as the breadwinner, had to be kept fit. It was a man's world, for as long as his strength lasted.

Strong faces and determination. These men in their own steadfast way defied the sea and for years, through sheer hard work, prevented the ocean from flooding one of England's successful iron ore mines.

Early mining attempts in the Hodbarrow area near Millom seemed to indicate that there was little to be found. The earl of Lonsdale tried in the 1840s but gave up looking. The newly formed Hodbarrow Mining Company took over exploration, though many felt it was a waste of time and would come to little. What happened exceeded everyone's expectations.

In 1856 the company discovered a solid mass of ore. It was so rich a deposit that a decade later more than 250 Cumbrian and Cornish miners were working under-ground and great quantities were being dug out. More excitement arose as the company realised that a further mass of ore extended under the Duddon Estuary. This deposit stretched enticingly for an unknown distance. But there were difficulties. As the miners tunneled closer towards the high-water mark, the danger of subsidence and flooding grew, and the company decided it needed to build a wall if it was going to keep out the sea.

In the end it took three walls. The first, in 1885, was a wooden barrier, but it was not enough. Soon a stronger more ambitious wall was started. It was a considerable success and rapidly allowed mining to extend seaward. Some four to five million tons of ore were dug out. Within a few years, however, alarming subsidence affected even this barrier. Emergency repairs were made, but more effort was needed if the mine were to be saved, and the company decided to build an even bigger wall, the Outer Barrier, as it became known. This giant construction was a mile and a quarter (2km) long, stretching from Haverigg to Hodbarrow Point. Massive indeed, it was made out of limestone rubble, slag and clay, and giant twenty-five ton concrete blocks. It loomed some sixteen feet (5m) above the men.

Thanks to these walls, the life of Hodbarrow was greatly extended and millions of tons of ore were dug out successfully. In the end, though, output began to decline, and while there were folk in Millom who sometimes said there must surely be more ore out there only waiting to be found, in the 1960s the great mine closed. With the shutdown of the pumps, Hodbarrow flooded. Today the Outer Barrier encloses a huge lake, a sanctuary for wildfowl and seabirds, and men who gave their all to wrest the iron from the land are a memory now in a vivid photograph.

Aspatria miners prepare to return to the surface as their shift ends deep down in no 4 pit, Brayton Domain collieries. Coal and Aspatria were once synonymous. Mention one and you thought of the other. The old mining communities lay round the town in a rich embrace. A first in a series of pits was sunk in 1850, and over the years others followed, with the last, the no 5, between Ellen Villa and Arkleby, reaching down more than 1,000 feet (330m).

They trudged through dark mine tunnels alongside the men, 600 feet (180m) down, hauling coal wagons along wet rails, with names like Den, Jumpy, Laddo and Shy Sam. The Brayton pit ponies, their stables below ground, worked unseen by the world above where the home fires were burning.

The harshness of farm life can readily be sensed in the face of this woman as she poses with a primitive handcart in north Cumberland. However, she is well wrapped up. Her outfit includes clogs, a bonnet, a skirt with deep tucks, and a shawl — which has one of her few concessions to decoration, tassels. The large coarse apron, or *brat*, could usually be bought in shops, though most women saved money by making their own out of meal bags.

Trowels ready, builders and their foreman take a break during restoration work on a house near Stainton, Penrith. If safety helmets are not yet in, caps always were.

The capable face of servant authority, 1900. This housekeeper who worked in Windermere poses with her lace knitting and displays just a few frills of her own, including a wedding ring, centre-parted hair and a cameo brooch. At her waist is the symbol of her authority, a large key-ring and keys to the laundry cupboard, the linen chest, the larder and usually all the cupboards in the house barring the master's and mistress's desks. A house-keeper's qualities had to include not only the ability to manage young servant girls, but also to appear just a little bit plainer than the mistress. Beautiful hair had to be tucked away, and smiles, particularly in the direction of the master, likewise had to be restrained. That, at least, was what was expected.

One job often regarded as a step up in the social scale was to find work as a maid in an hotel, or as a waiter in the case of men, positions usually obtained by word of mouth recommendation, or through hiring agencies. Young girls at least could thus avoid farm work and the indignity of standing in a street at the twice-yearly hirings. Here is the smartly dressed staff at the Old England, Bowness, Windermere, with authority apparent at several levels, and that of Mrs Richards, seated in the centre, definitely paramount.

Stone by stone, a drystone waller works on a snowy fell, repairing a gap. Hundreds of walls encompass the Cumbrian mountains, most of them built in the eighteenth or nineteenth centuries, though others may reach back a thousand years. Some mark a parish or a landowner's boundary, others record an attempt to win a few more acres from the fells, while a few seem to hint at some purpose long since forgotten. Often they look as old as the stone circles, out of which sometimes came the pieces from which they were built. An advantage of drystone walls is that water has less effect than on a mortared wall, which can be washed out. A disadvantage is that drystone walls are draughtier.

Stone Walling at Lorton.

To be Let,

BY PROPOSAL,

At the GLOBE INN, in
COCKERMOUTH,

On MONDAY the 28th Day of APRIL, Instant,
At Six o'Clock in the Afternoon,

(In such Lots as may then be fixed,)

The Getting STONES

AND ERECTING

A WALL

ON LORTON COMMON,

Beginning at High Swinside, and extending along Swinside Fell to Lady Seat Pike, and by Hope Doors to Hob Carton Craggs.

JOSEPH ROBINSON, of Armaside in Lorton, will shew the Line of Walling, and the Conditions as to the Heights, &c. of the Wall will be produced at the Time of Letting; and further Particulars may in the mean time be known on applying to Mr. HUDLESTON, of Gosforth, the Commissioner for inclosing Lorton Common.

9th APRIL, 1828.

THOMAS BAILEY, PRINTER, COCKERMOUTH.

The noise of racing drive-belts and whirling wheels made lip reading a considerable asset in bobbin mills. Typically, the floor of this one is a fireman's nightmare and deep in wood shavings. Forty-nine bobbin mills once existed in Lakeland and great numbers of bobbins were produced, particularly for the North's cotton and woollen mills, but as the industries declined the mills closed. Here boring and turning are under way with good strong swill baskets to hold the finished bobbins.

A bogey loaded with clogs of slate is ready for pushing into the cutting shed at Hodge Close Green Slate Quarry, Tilberthwaite Valley. This was before diamond-tipped saws, so the clogs would be split by hammer and chisel — *riving* it is called — each piece making ten or a dozen slates. On the right is Bob Walker, and on the left a quarry owner, Claud Cann.

Many roofs in the North of England are clad in Lakeland slate, as well as numerous buildings elsewhere, including New Scotland Yard in London. Even further afield, in Boston, United States, a proud American once showed me the front of a building which had been faced with green slate. 'That's from your British Lake District', he informed me. And it was, beautiful, and green and durable.

Ask a quarryman how long Hodge Close slate lasts, and the answer will be a good 200 years, perhaps longer. No one has lived 200 years to be absolutely sure. That's what they'll tell you.

The metal is red-hot as the men at Old Hutton, Kendal, lift the hoop from the fire. A few steps and it will be lowered onto the waiting wooden wheel on the hooping plate. Then there will be smoke and steam, and fast, careful work. Hoops were hammered into position, the hoopers pouring water, gauging the heat, ensuring the expanded metal shrank evenly until it nipped and left the finished wheel well balanced. Nor, in all this, must the wood be set ablaze. It is skilled work, requiring good judgement. Black-smiths made the metal hoops, joiners the wheels. Some hoopers, as at Oxen Park in High Furness, had a shallow hooping well into which they dropped the wheel to cool it quickly. The result, a wheel good for many a mile.

Peat cutters at work in the Lyth Valley. Huge belts of peat in Cumbria were worked for centuries until overtaken by coal. Many cottages and farms had turbary rights — the right to cut turf or peat for winter fuel, and some possibly still do. Slow-burning peat was often a vital part of a family's economy.

Nor is there anything quite like the two sweet scents of peat, the rich plum cake aroma when the brown slices are first cut, and the sweet smoke stealing across the fields on a cold night.

During a good drying year, the whole process, from cutting the first block to stacking, could be finished in five to six weeks. In most normal English summers, though, it usually took longer. In a bad year, especially in Lakeland, it might be autumn before the peat was all safely stacked and eventually carted away, in the case seen here, to sell in Kendal or to farms and cottages.

Peat rights were often carefully conserved and sometimes were the subject of bitter quarrels by rival claimants. Frequently the diggings were under the control of the old manorial courts, and this helped to ensure that the diggings were left in a tidy working state. Peat was regarded as an essential fuel, especially where homes were well away from the coal-producing areas. In a good year cottagers and farmers might succeed in 'graving' or cutting sufficient peats to last a year, or even longer.

Some old peat bogs, as in the Rusland Valley, High Furness (see opposite), are now rare and are appreciated for their wildlife rather than as a source of fuel. Those that are left are protected as Sites of Special Scientific Interest in recognition of their special plants and animals. In Cumbria the main SSSI peatlands are at Lyth, Haverthwaite and on the Solway Plain.

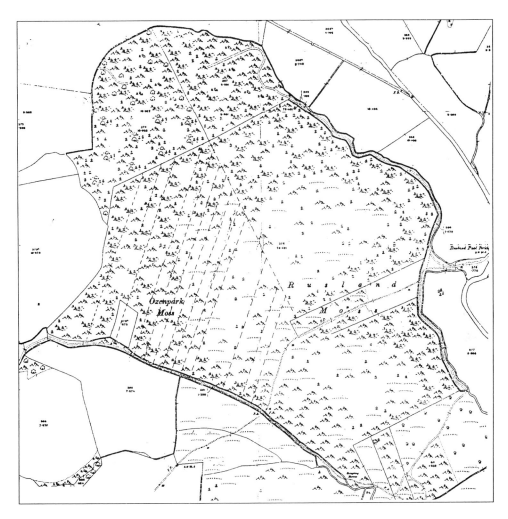

Rusland Moss when peat cutting took place in the Rusland Valley, High Furness. The moss is a raised mire, or peat bog. It formed after the end of the last Ice Age 10,000 to 7,000 years ago, and its underlying sands, gravels and clays show that it was once part of a tidal valley. Rusland Valley Mosses is regarded by its protectors, English Nature, as special for it is one of the few remaining lowland raised mires in all Britain and is unusual in that it lies at a valley head. Most sites are in coastal areas.

Some unusual or uncommon species are found at Rusland including sundew, which catches insects and then digests them, royal fern, large heath butterfly, and rare spiders and beetles. I once met an adder sunning itself on one of the moss paths, and gave it right of way.

The Oxenpark part of the moss relates to the hamlet a little to the south, where many of the dwellings could each cut peat for fuel from its own strip. In hard times this was a much-prized and valuable asset. Today the mosses are a Site of Special Scientific Interest and are protected under the Wildlife and Countryside Act 1981. Peat cutting, farming and forestry mean that ninety-four per cent of the original area of lowland raised mire in Britain have been lost. Hence Rusland's importance.

Opposite:

Meet a gold miner — well, *almost* a gold miner. The old Cumbrian look of long ago has rarely been better caught than in this picture of William and Sarah Leyland, taken by Maysons of Keswick outside the Leylands' home at Hollows Farm, Grange in Borrowdale.

In the 1840s the high-spirited William set out from his home near Barrow-in-Furness for Australia to try to make his fortune gold mining. He was hardly twenty years old and full of adventure. And he did find gold, but alas no fortune, just enough to make into a few rings and trinkets.

Home he came in his grand hat, and soon had found himself a girl, Sarah Wren, whose forebears had dwelt at Longthwaite Farm for decades. They married, and William wanted Sarah to return to the wilds of Australia but she was apprehensive about the sea, and in the end they settled for Lakeland.

Sarah and William successfully worked a farm and a quarry at Rigg Head in Borrowdale. Sarah, who could read and write, did the accounts; William ran the quarry and the farm. They were well liked, and sold slate far and wide. The couple lived into their seventies and had three boys and three girls. William never went back to look for more gold, but throughout his life he often wore his Australian hat with the flap turned up, perhaps as a reminder of his gold-rush days.

A pick and shovel gang near Ambleside. Their task can only be guessed at, but it looks messy and no one's risking getting their hair dirty.

Joe Grisenthwaite's smithy near the New Hall Inn — the present Hole in t' Wall — Bowness, Windermere, c1895. This smithy was opposite Jossy Wray's where Sam Hoggarth, whose story is opposite, started as an apprentice.

Two coach horses are being shod, and displayed on the board are some of the shoes which were used for different foot ailments. If a horse's sole came down, for instance, then a wide-webbed shoe would be used to keep it off the ground.

For generations, blacksmiths were important members of any rural community. A century ago when Grisenthwaite's smithy was active, hundreds of blacksmiths thrived in the county. In the summer months especially, horses and their minders were often to be seen queueing outside the smithies waiting to be shod, sometimes as late as nine or ten o' clock at night. The horses had to be fit and ready for work the next morning.

Inside the smithy was a twilight world of smoke-begrimed windows and blackened walls, rapidly transformed to a ruddy glow once the bellows were pumped and the hearth flared into life. Still more light as horseshoes were heated white-hot and hammered on an anvil, the sparks flying into the gloom.

Shoeing a horse was to see a craftsman at work. First the horse had to learn who was the master. A good blacksmith was not only strong, he also gave the horse confidence by his own self-assurance. And the horse, when all was done and it had been reshod, would stamp the ground as if to test the fit.

Blacksmiths filled a useful role in the community in many ways. They could repair harrows, ploughs and chains, and mend or make a host of other items including sickles, spades and building tools. New bottoms for the fire grate, oven shelves, gate hoops, hinges and heaters for irons, all would be tackled. They even patched kettles.

Blacksmith Sam Hoggarth was a giant of a man, broad shouldered and extremely strong. He was born in 1892 and lived at Sawrey, near Hawkshead, one of a family of nine children. In 1906 he started work aged fourteen as an apprentice blacksmith at Jossy Wray's in Bowness, Windermere, and later in life he had his own smithy at Lindale, near Grange-over-Sands. He worked every day of the year except Good Friday ...

Well I allus fancied being a blacksmith. For one thing I liked horses. Started when I was fourteen at Bowness, Windermere, that is for a feller called Jossy Wray. In 1906. There were two smithies in t'lane, us and Joe Grisenthwaite's opposite. I began as an apprentice. It was a good job to be a smith. Take me father, a waller ... he's come home many a time with only five shillings [25p] for t'week because they were rained off ... and there were eleven mouths to feed, eleven of us! Well a blacksmith was never rained off, you were in a good job, under cover. I told my father that.

I'd four brothers and four sisters. My father would be out of work seventeen weeks in that big frost [the Great Freeze, 1894-5]; and I once says to him: 'How did you manage, father?' And he says: 'Nay, I don't know, lad. A lot of folk had to go to t'workhouse.'

When I started at blacksmiths I used to cross the lake in the ferry, it were a row boat; and then walk on to Bowness, landing at work twenty-past seven. Finished five-thirty. I got six shilling [30p] a week; four shilling for mother; one for my ferry fares; and a shilling for meself.

I was only nailing on at start off, and others did the fitting. Shoed me first horse at fifteen. I was right proud of that!

We were shoeing horses for the Old England Hotel. In winters there'd be Bob Mackerell shoeing and Bob Aitken. They started at eight; shoeing the bus horses for up to Windermere and the station. I used to put in the sharps, for getting a hold on ice.

At Grisenthwaite's there used to be Jack Redman — old Jack. Whenever the boss went out, quick as owt Jack would slip round to the pub to get a pint — and down it like that! Well some fellers knew when he was coming one day and they put a mouse in his pint. Dead of course. Well Jack ran round and they says: 'There's one there, Jack'. And Jack downed it in one go. Downed it and says: 'There was a bloody good hop in that!'

I stayed at Bowness with Jossy till eighteen; then on to Isaac Wilson's up at Windermere, till twenty-one.

We had mebbe six horses to shoe perhaps before our breakfast. We started at six there. I was an improver by then. We did a lot of coach horses, on the Keswick run they was. There was three of us working. We did any horse there was — fishmonger's, butcher's, milk feller, everybody had a horse then; grocer's, all the grocers. And there were cart horses, farm horses. We had 'em all through the day. In winter we had fewer to shoe, but spent time making new shoes. It was up to four shillings for shoeing a horse then, all round. A lot of money. Thinking about it, life was grand in them days.

Well the war came and I went into the army, field artillery, working with mules in France as a first-class shoeing specialist. When we was advancing, I had fifty-six of my mules killed, you know, with shelling. All at once. We were in a big shell hole. A shell landed and we got out. The mules caught it.

But they's beggars to shoe. When you shoes 'em they look round to see where you're at … to kick you. Well one upped with its hind foot, catching me in t'face, knocked me over. Next thing, I'd grabbed it, right mad I was, and threw it into a muck midden. Well I was strong then!

When I come out of the war I started on me own at Lindale, near Grange-over-Sands. It was sixteen shilling [80p] to shoe a farm horse, what was once only four. Lindale was a place I was at most of me life after that. Plenty of work.

I used to have horses to shoe as was never broken in; I used to shout at 'em. They were frightened when I shouted, often enough. 'Get UP!' I'd shout. It's the voice as does it. When I used to shout at a horse it behaved different. Getting hold of it was important. Matter of who was boss. Of course I could hold 'em. Could happen get a bad horse, take a bit longer then. Kicked around a bit. One racehorse out of Cartmel kicked me up the arse a dozen times.

I could go on … But one thing I'll tell on: I never drove a nail in on a Good Friday, not on any horse 'cause when Christ was crucified it was blacksmith as would have ta make t'nails, happen that same day as they was used, and they would have ta be droven. I've never made any nails for driving on a Good Friday. You'd not have me nailing Christ to t'cross.

When I were a lad, everyone depended on t' blacksmith. Doest know story of King Solomon's palace? Well he gives all t' men who built it a grand feast. A proper do. And efter a bit, king says to first 'un:

'And what's it with thee?'

'Oh, well, king, I built t' walls'.

'Aye?' says Solomon. 'Grand! And who sharpens the tools?'

'Oh', he says, 'well, t' blacksmith does.'

And king asks another: 'And what's it with thee?'

'Oh, I's a joiner. I did t' joinery'.

'Aye?' says king. 'And who sharpens the tools?'

'Well', he says, 't' blacksmith.'

And Solomon went on down the table till he comes to t' last un: 'And what's it with thee?'

'Well, I's a blacksmith', says the man.

'Oh yes', says king, 'and who sharpens the tools?'

'Well … I does', he says.

'Oh, aye, and where'd you get 'em in fust place?' says the king.

'Why', says t' blacksmith, 'I meks 'em.'

Then Solomon in a big voice says: 'Aaay, get thee ta top of t' table! Without thee there'd be no work for any of these devils!'

The motor age is coming ... The scale of Christopher Wilson's thinking at Lindale, Grange-over-Sands, can be gathered by this illustration which embraces a garage, a motor works, cars and smoking chimneys, all to show which way the wind was blowing.

C. WILSON & SONS,

CARRIAGE
BUILDERS,

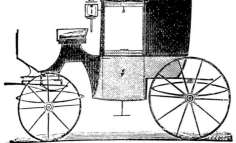

Lightburne Works,
ULVERSTON,
AND
LINDALE, GRANGE-over-SANDS.

ANY DESIRED STYLE OF
RUBBER TYRES Fitted (Sections submitted).

ELECTRIC AND ACETYLENE LAMPS.

A good selection of
CARRIAGES & ACCESSORIES
always in stock.

**ALL MATERIAL CAREFULLY SELECTED
AND WELL SEASONED.**

Fishermen stand poised in the Solway with *haaf nets*, and wait for the approach of unsuspecting salmon and sea trout. Before getting in line, the men draw lots for their positions and then stand often waist-deep holding the nets firmly in the flow.

Haaf fishing, which is still practised, could be a thousand years old and a legacy from the Vikings. The fishermen's use of the old method of *casting the mell* — or drawing lots — to try to win the best position in the line is said to date from those times, while the word 'haaf' is related to Old Norse.

Each net has a frame about sixteen feet by five (5m x 1.5m) and though of light construction it needs strength, as well as considerable skill, to use one properly. Once in position, each fisherman holds a short handle-length of wood, pushes the middle pole down into the sand and the net billows out with the flowing water in a long tail, its open mouth awaiting the oncoming shoals.

Farm and Fell

CLOGS AND COBBLES, middens and mud, and a ripe old stench — that is how it was in many a Cumbrian farmyard in 1900. A hundred years on, there are still places a bit like that, the mud at least, but it was a frequent condition in those days, as many a farmer watching a Lakeland deluge from the shelter of his barn doorway will tell you.

Cast-iron water pumps with long curved handles stood out in the yard; or there was a well, or a spring down the *lonning* or lane. Luckier places had a tap just outside at the back door. Primitive privies — the *nettie*, *nessie* or water closet — sulked across the yard, one- and two-seaters, sometimes even three holes in a row, side by side, sociably, the long wooden seat scrubbed a bleached white.

For many, electricity seemed a world away, perhaps not even dreamed of; candles and paraffin oil lamps lit most Lakeland farmhouses and byres. Milking was by hand from five or six o'clock onwards; with the eggs to collect, the pig and the geese to feed, the cows to set out to pasture, the horses to harness, the byre to muck out, and the resulting steaming heap dumped on the muck heap ready for carting, to leave in piles before it was spread on the land. Scaling the muck, that's the phrase.

When stock was sold it was early away, on foot, driving sheep or cattle to the markets in the distant towns, Carlisle, Cockermouth, Penrith, Kendal, Ulverston and elsewhere. Just about everybody walked. Most had to. Thought nothing of it. Often the sale animals arrived at the auction town the night before and were lodged at farms handy for an early start. Farmers might send sons ahead as drovers, which usefully left a hired hand free. Many a young Cumbrian has set out to walk with a flock of trotting sheep on the evening before a sale, and driven them miles before his father has caught up by pony and cart and taken over.

Sale day, and stock sold at auction would be sent on its way by the new owners, perhaps by rail, but often walked, often far, at an agreed price by one of the rough-looking drovers who drifted around the mart watching for work. Typical were those at Penrith: Piggy Willy, Dirty Dick, Old Whackham, Candy Jack and others … their names made sweet rough music. Most were lucky if they earned 3s 6d (17½p) a week.

For a sixpence (2½p) a drover would prepare a farmer's cows for the sale, washing and brushing them, scraping their horns with broken glass, and rubbing them down with oil so that the beasts entered the ring shining with health. The drovers were a wild lot, and many among them knew their own peg numbers in Carlisle jail.

A century ago the number of people working on the land was greater than today. Many farms had hired hands, unlike recent times when farms have often been run by the 'Last Ditch Trio' — the farmer, his wife and their tractor. As a comparison, in 1900 a farm, depending on its size, might be expected to feed a family of four: in recent years it came down to one person, though with BSE and foot and mouth, not even that. Many farming families have had to find work elsewhere — gardening, cleaning, odd-jobbing. Sons and daughters move on.

And there was another difference. 'The countryside', an old lengthman told me, 'was *tidy* then.' Drystone walls were in better repair, hedges neater, fields often smaller; and the bracken — creeping back into old kingdoms and choking the grazing — was held at bay, effectively cut in annual purges, providing bedding for byres and boxes. On the roads there were many more lengthmen who filled in potholes as soon as they were seen, with mud and stone chippings if with nothing else; grass verges, too, were trimmed back, and left in long straight lines which other roadmen eyed up and commented on whether it was a good job or not.

Tidy, the countryside, but altering. Even slow-to-change Cumberland and Westmorland began to see mechanical reapers around, and mowing machines, hay rakes, tedders, oil-cake breakers, pulpers, grinding mills and double-furrow ploughers.

For many in the three old Lakeland counties of Cumberland, Westmorland and North Lancashire that make up Cumbria, animals were at the centre of farming, with sheep the main provider. Yet one of the most important animals on the farm was not necessarily the bread-winning Herdwick, nor the Rough Fell nor the marvellous Swaledale sheep, but the working horse. Every farm needed horses. Clydesdales and Shires were greatly favoured. And they were cared for. To lose a horse was a tragedy, for it was not only a good worker but also a loyal friend, one you came to know and to trust, just as it came to know you. There was an earthy side, too: 'I'd rather hear a horse fart than hear the vicar preach in Latin' — that goes back a long way. So it was horse power at the plough for potato and turnip crops; horses on the fell to drag bracken sleds for cattle bedding; horses pulling the mowers, the farmer lurching along on a high metal seat, padded with sacking, little imagining that one day horses would be replaced.

The canniest Cumbrians in 1900 were the Herdwicks. These tough, marvellous mountain sheep managed to survive along with Swaledales on windswept fells where other breeds might perish. Ewes, trapped and buried in snowdrifts for as long as two weeks (some farmers tell of three), have been dug out alive and, miraculously it seems, have still given birth at next lambing time.

For an age, the pattern of gathering sheep, tupping, lambing, washing and hand clipping went on unbroken, with clipping time one of the important events in the Cumbrian farm calendar. Even forty years ago it was still common for farmers and their labourers to visit each neighbouring farm in turn with hand-shears at the ready to help out on clipping days. Once the men had dealt with the mutton, then the women showed what could be done with the beef. Come evening, the tables were laden with sizzling joints, jacket potatoes, pease pudding, dumplings, oat bread, apple pie and much else; talk, songs and a wealth of hunting tales followed; and a jug of strong brew went the rounds.

Some changes on the farm were enforced. Until 1905 there were Herdwicks and fell flocks still being salved with rancid butter and Stockholm tar. The evil-smelling mix discouraged parasites, the lice, the ticks, the keds; but it was slow work. Patiently the salve was rubbed into each animal, a handful at a time. Salving twelve sheep was a day's work for one man — and farms could run from fifty to a thousand sheep. Then sheep dip became compulsory, and was quicker and cheaper.

Fell farmers often kept a few cattle, though in general it was the Cumbrian lowlander with richer grazing whose herds were the largest. A common sight were the beautifully coloured Cumberland Shorthorns, proudly described as *the* breed of cattle in the North, perhaps in all England. Apparently in the 1880s it nearly died out, but men whose fathers and grandfathers had kept the breed saved it. Red, roan, or white, Cumberland Shorthorns seemed a part of the land.

Many rural households used to fatten a pig, especially the Cumberland pig, now extinct; there were more bulls; and many folk kept a goose or two. The last were bought off neighbours, or at market, or each summer from passing Irish drovers, the birds fattened on the corn stubble in time for Christmas,.

Milk yields were lower; likewise crop yields; and even hay was claimed by some to have been less valuable at the century's turn than turnips, because eating turnips off by sheep was seen as a valuable way of improving the land. But hay is such a good crop. An early start, the farmers up at 5am before the heat of day, before the *clegs* (horseflies) begin to bite, and the satisfaction when it was a good year and the hay was in, the sweet hay.

In late summer came harvesting. Plenty of oats. In earlier times, harvesting had meant reaping with the sickle, and the scythe, busy teams of workers lifting and binding the sheaves. Tradesmen, artisans, whole families turned out to help with the corn harvest. The sheaves were stooked and stayed in the fields until dry, perhaps for two or three Sundays.

The spread of horse-drawn reaping machines gradually put paid to most sickles and scythes, though not completely, for even in Edwardian times one could still see some in use. It was hard work. Cutting lasted from morning till night, and when the work had finished at one farm, the casuals moved on to start over again at another.

Mechanisation increased. And so, quite suddenly it seemed, there were farmers buying, or thinking of buying, the latest marvels — reaping machines, and self-binders. It took only two men to operate the reaper, one for the horse and one to put off the load, and only one for the self-binder. For many casual workers it spelled disaster. Fewer men and women were needed. The farmer's family and their hired hands could often manage the whole job themselves.

The part played by the horse seemed unchallenged, though the steam ploughs of 1907 were certainly emerging. Leading the harvest by horse was still a customary sight, loaded carts bumping homewards from distant fields. High shelvings or wooden sides were fitted to increase capacity, and if there were no shelvings, then the sheaves were skilfully built into the carts so that the load was balanced and stayed in place. Too heavy, at one end or the other, made it harder for the horse.

At the stack more hard work, more pitch-forking, some eight or ten loads to each stack, and the whole thing to thatch against the wet, often beautifully done. Dutch barns made the job easier, but that needed money, and a long depression in farming, starting back in the 1870s, was hitting hard in places. Other depressions were to follow, including the 1920s, the 1930s and the cruel times of today.

Threshing day … and steam gained ground. The old horse-drawn threshing machines, worked in a gin case, were ousted by the awesome travelling traction engines.

Come mid-October and the farmyard filled with the exciting noise of turning wheels and rippling drive belts. A cartload of coal lay piled on the cobbles; a gang of labourers raced to feed the machinery. Strangely, the new marvel sometimes needed more men than the old barn threshers, perhaps ten or eleven hands for efficient working, the key man now being the engine driver. Two men forked the sheaves to the machine, another hand cut the bands, one fed the drum and likely there was a trusser, two others to stack, another to take off the corn sacks; and two to cart the corn to the granary, as well as keep the thirsty engine dosed with water. Plenty of ripe banter around, too, and the threshers' lungs as dusty as ever.

Lowland farms saw the thresher first, then the machines moved up the fellsides and valleys from farm to farm. At some spots, threshing was over by mid-November, but at others two perhaps three threshings took place, before Christmas and after.

Clogs and cobbles, and middens and mud — it seemed ever thus.

Jim Dixon farmed at Town End, Grasmere, and was able to wield this long-shafted scythe for hours on end and still maintain a good, even, quality cut. He took pride in being able to slice down a field of hay and leave no visible joins in the lines of stubble.

Farmhands at Godmans Hall Farm, Burneside, rake the hay into cocks.

The hard-working Mossop sisters of Rogerscale near Cockermouth pause in a field in clogs and working clothes. Both apparently are in farm work, but everything is not what it seems, for while one was a farmer, the other was a schoolteacher at the hamlet of Dean, living at home mainly at weekends. Their old farm had a magnificent oak settle that was the talk of the neighbourhood, while round the cast-iron fire range was a railway coach wheel as a fender. There was no inside water supply so the sisters carried it from a well in buckets, using a yoke. The sisters were well liked, though which one do you suppose was the teacher? The person who lent the picture could not remember, but she knew that one of them was.

Loading the hay in the Stubbing Field at Howgill Farm, Sebergham. On the top of the load is farmer Thomas Stobart. On the left, his daughter Annie complete with a cloutie bonnet, centre is young Wilfrid Stobart, and right, a hired hand.

A good many things have disappeared from Cumbria, and among them is the Cumberland pig. This lusty porker, Sally, was once in a class of her own, arrived at down many years of domestic pig breeding and greatly prized by our forefathers who enjoyed fat meat — indeed, the fatter the pig, the better they seemed to like it.

Sally was reported to be the last pure-bred Cumberland pig. Years ago, many rural households in Cumbria fattened a pig each year for butchering. Poorer families depended on it, for pigs, it is often said, have no waste 'except', as the wits remind us, 'for the grunt'. Another saying was that while hens and (poached) rabbits kept the family fed, the pig paid the rent.

The Cumberland pig was rather shorter in the body than the modern commercial porker, and it was chubbier faced. After the First World War the Cumberland was expected to help in the upsurge in commercial pork production. Its breeders were convinced that no better animal could be found in all Britain. In 1921, Newton Rigg Farm School established a pedigree herd of Cumberland Pigs; and there was a Cumberland Pig Breeders' Association with more than 300 members. The future of the breed seemed assured. But the Cumberland was doomed. It lost favour. The Landrace and the Large White, and the crosses between them, helped to displace the old Cumberland.

Sally was owned by Thomas Thirlwall of Bothel Craggs, near Cockermouth. Anxious to maintain the breed, he searched the country for a boar to mate her, but he came to the conclusion that no true Cumberland boar was available and the breed became extinct.

Shepherding on the heights.

The Jacksons of Uzzicar Farm, Newlands Valley, proudly show off their dairy Shorthorns. The middle cow, Lady Derwent, won a silver cup and was sold to a Liverpool
buyer for 100 guineas, a considerable sum at the time, 1898. Shorthorns at one time
were widespread in the North, doing well on poor pasture and having a good
reputation as a strong, dual-purpose cow. But you can't win. For some farmers they
did not produce enough milk, while others regarded them as too fat for beef. In the
end, fashion changed and in general they went out of favour.

Often sheep were washed before being clipped, as at Langwathby Bridge on the River Eden. They were kept swimming round in the water a time or two to get all the sand, grease and dirt out, and this improved the value of the wool, which was worth a good deal more washed than unwashed. Then the fleeces went to the woollen mills. Today special processes with chemicals are used to clean the wool which is sold to the mills.

Opposite:

A boon clipping day at Little Langdale. At full pitch, bleating and shouts fill the yard as one by one the ewes are brought kicking and struggling to the clippers who squat on stools. And almost before the sheep know it, each is grabbed and, amid a rapid click-clicking of hand shears, its fleece is speedily pared from its body. Constant cries ring out: 'marker!' when an identifying *rudd* or tar mark is put on; 'catcher!' the moment the next ewe is wanted; and, less welcome, 'lime!' if an unlucky ewe suffers a cut. At once a lad runs with the lime bucket to dab the wound.

Frequent moments of confusion erupt and plaintive baaing as lambs race round the yard searching for their newly clipped mothers, now strangely whitish and no longer a familiar comforting smell. More baas, too, as a ewe escapes and belts into the crowd. Plenty is going on.

If a man could take the wool from eight to nine sheep in an hour he was reckoned a useful hand, though some are reputed to have worked faster than that. Some sheep clip better than others. An exceptionally good man, it has been said, has clipped a record three ewes in seven or eight minutes. Some going. Styles varied from the round clip, like apples, to the quicker long clip, a bit like peeling bananas. Whichever method, the fleeces were seized by the women, rolled and stored awaiting sale.

The women's work had started days before, preparing to feed the clippers. At some farms up to forty or fifty men might turn up to help. Ham would be boiled, and a Herdwick wether shearling killed ready for the dinner at night; one about eighteen months old was acknowledged to have the best flavour.

The clippers usually got a first bite to eat at noon. Ham or jam sandwiches went out in baskets; rolled gingerbread, rock buns and fruit cake. Unsweetened tea in enamel mugs. Then more clipping till the next break while the women prepared dinner for six o'clock or so. At some farms the Herdwick wether would be cut down the middle, and then across. Four pieces out of one sheep for carving; or there would be a giant roast, cabbage and potatoes; and in the set pot, ginger and sultana puddings steaming towards perfection.

As a precaution, knowing farmers' wives tied sacking round table legs to prevent the men's clogs and boots from kicking the furniture to bits. Come dinner, the beer barrel was broached, and songs and laughter filled the night.

Rough Fell Sheep before and after clipping at Ivy House, Selside. Their wool, almost down to the ground, is coarse, and the fleeces off these two Lakeland worthies probably ended as carpets or mats. Carpet wool needs to be springy, tough, resilient and warm. Clips off Rough Fells are usually considered to be ideal.

Opposite:
Fifteen of the twenty women who kept everyone fed at the annual sheep clipping at Glencoin Farm, Patterdale, in 1906. It is Wednesday the 4th July, and more than seventy people gathered in the farmyard to help the Wilkinson family clip the wool off 2,000 sheep. Neighbours had walked in from miles around to help. Starting soon after seven in the morning, the task took nine hours, and the women seen here not only kept the clippers going with refreshments during the day, they also prepared a giant meal for the evening. By day-end a hundred people were involved. On this occasion, many excursion visitors also arrived. They had travelled especially from Blackburn to see how the wool on their backs was won.

A busy moment at Red Mire Farm, Mungrisdale. Farmer John Bleasdale holds a newly clipped Swaledale ewe which has just been marked by his son Joseph with a hot tar *smit mark*, a crow's foot.

Farmers use a variety of methods to recognise their sheep, such as red, blue or black pop marks, initials or other combinations. Sheep also get *lug marks*, their ears clipped so they are recognisable. Sometimes horns are branded. Smit marks can be found in *Shepherds' Guides* books, which are updated from time to time. Smit daubs in some areas were made by boiling grease with Venetian Red and tar. Often the tar was heated at the fireside, and one memorable day way back, one of the Bleasdales' neighbours, a grandmother renowned for her professed immobility, was crouching at the hearth when the bubbling pot caught fire. The old woman did not wait for help, but grabbed up her skirts and ran from the house, yelling as she went, evidently cured.

Young Ned Nelson, veteran sheep farmer, sits it out in the sheepfold at Gatesgarth Farm with a Herdwick ram lamb. For three-quarters of a century Ned kept Herdwicks towards the head of Buttermere Valley. He lived into the 1930s to the age of eighty-seven, and was renowned as a breeder, exhibitor and judge of these tough mountain sheep.

Yet there is another Ned to this story — his father, old Ned Nelson, whose claim to fame was in some ways greater than his son's, for it was he who built up the flock to a high standard of excellence and helped to bring Lakeland's Herdwicks to a degree they had not previously enjoyed.

Several good stories exist about the origin of Herdwicks. There are strong advocates that they were washed ashore from a ship stranded at Ravenglass, perhaps from the Spanish Armada. Equally strong in their views are those who believe the breed arrived still earlier with the Norse settlers, though even that may not be true, appealing though the idea is. Nowadays many say that the Cumbrian mountains were well populated before the Norse appeared by indigenous flocks of tough, wily, agile mountain sheep, out of the Bronze Age or Neolithic times, and which were taken over by the Norse settlers and developed. No one knows for sure, though many now accept the last view.

Old Ned, the kindly over-generous farmer, for that was his reputation, settled into Gatesgarth as a tenant possessed by a kind of dream, to turn the poor relation of all other sheep, the Herdwick, into a prizewinner. Gatesgarth was ideal for his experiment. It had 180 inside acres (73ha), 800 acres (325ha) fell land, and a sheep run along the tops four miles (6.5km) in one direction and eight (9km) the other, making a total of about 3,000 acres (1,200ha). The stock taken over with the tenancy numbered 400 Herdwick ewes, plus *hoggets* (young sheep before its first clipping), *shearlings* (young sheep after its first clipping) and *wethers* (young castrated lamb), in all 1,744 sheep. With these, Ned started a careful, selective breeding programme and set about showing the best of them in the show rings.

Almost disbelief, indeed scorn greeted Ned's Herdwicks when they first ran into the rings. Buyers were quick to point out their smallness and lack of meat. But old Ned persisted and in 1836 at Egremont he won his first prize. The stock improved slowly, and though many still spoke disparagingly, he began to win more often. Judges tended to prefer lowland sheep to the fellsiders. Ned, though, was patient and in 1864, to the amazement of the doubters, his ram, Thousand-a-Year, won the champion at the Royal Show in Newcastle. Success indeed. Winning prizes at distant shows became Ned's obsession, and eventually his vastly improved Herdwicks swept all before them. At Gatesgarth his trophy walls became layers deep in prize tokens.

It has been said that thanks to old Ned Nelson, and no doubt to others like him, the Herdwick came into its own as a breed, though it was never as popular elsewhere as in Lakeland. The heart of this story, though, is not Ned's undeniable success, nor his son's follow-on in the shepherding tradition, but the Ned Nelsons as men. Father and son were as close as one could get to the heart of this mountainous land, two Cumbrians in their element.

Farmers in caps, judges in hard hats, the sheep in a pensive line. It's a critical moment as the experts examine a line of ewes at Hesket Newmarket show, 1908.

Agricultural College, Aspatria.

Stern looking and Victorian, this is Aspatria Agricultural College, the fount of a remarkable revolution in Cumbria. The leading man in the enterprise, the college principal, Henry J Webb, among the many farming challenges he tackled, courageously set out to teach Cumbrian farmers' wives how to make butter. At the time there were those who regarded this proposal as outrageous, for every farmer's wife in the county sincerely believed that her butter was already the best. The facts, however, suggested otherwise.

Dr Webb was not exactly thrilled at what he saw as the Cumbrian scene, where new modes of agriculture were often slow to take root. He had been surprised to find that Cumbrian butter was selling in the markets for only sixpence (2½p) or so a pound, whereas Danish butter, wherever it was sold, fetched three times that price. When he examined and tasted Cumbrian butter he was surprised no longer: Danish butter was better in every way, and the shrewd doctor started his campaign.

Uniformity was what was required, uniformity in dairying methods such as in Denmark and Sweden. In Lakeland every farmer's wife had a different method of making butter; different in details, but those differences were sufficient to produce a Cumbrian butter, which on average was an inferior product.

Aspatria College was established in 1874, linked to the science departments of Queen Victoria's Educational Council and approved by many county councils who instituted scholarships tenable at the college. Its main aims were to teach practical and scientific farming.

It was not the only farm college to start up in Cumbria. In the 1890s, Newton Rigg Farm School was established near Penrith, and this too proved to be a success.

At Aspatria the college, after a bit of a struggle at first, gradually began to thrive. Its students, who included many drawn from different parts of the world, had a choice of instruction including how to be farmers, land agents, agricultural chemists and much else. The college also urged the use of new ways of stock breeding, and instructed how to use fertilisers and how to breed improve types of cattle, sheep and horses. Much was happening.

While butter making was only one aspect of the college's aims, Dr Webb was quick to see its importance to the Cumbrian economy. He calculated that its quality could be greatly improved so that it could become a major Cumbrian farm product, and not merely the by-product, which it then was. First he set out to encourage farmers to switch from the ancient breed of Longhorn cows to Ayrshires, Jerseys and Shorthorns, all of which he expected to give better results. He also decided to send his message out into the classrooms, taught by his sister Marion.

In 1899 the Travelling Dairy School, or the Migratory Dairy, was established. Equipped with a vehicle and a tent to hold twelve working pupils, along with all their utensils, it travelled round the villages and towns, and at each venue gave a ten-day course in butter making. Seventeen places were targeted, including Keswick, Wigton and Penrith, and many pupils joined the classes.

Butter churns ready, a dozen working pupils and a teacher stand ready to demonstrate in their dairy tent classroom how to make high-quality butter, one that will be better and cheaper than Danish imports.

It was a long task but eventually the travelling dairy had a noticeable effect. The day came when the old Cumbrian saying 'The more the salt, the better the butter' was no longer true. The new process was easy on salt and was undoubtedly making a better, sweeter butter of high quality. Temperature control, cleanliness, churning methods and a host of other simple butter-making rules helped to bring about the revolution. The market price of the new butter climbed to a shilling, then 1s 3d, until it became apparent that the Danes no longer had it all their own way.

The world-famed college at Aspatria, as the *Agricultural Economist* for 1900 described it, lasted until the First World War. Then it was robbed of its students who flocked to join up, and the college never fully revived. In the end, it was demolished and Beacon Hill School was built on the site.

Today, the county's other agricultural college, Newton Rigg, lives on and is administered by the university of Central Lancashire.

Dalston, 1906. The farming revolution in Cumberland is under way. Farmers and their families stare at the latest marvel in the agricultural world — the Ivel motor plough, a forerunner of the tractor. Few had been seen in the North of England at this time, and it was the first of its kind to be introduced into Cumberland. The machine was bought by Mr R Tinniswood of Rosebank, and the crowd is being shown how it can do a three-furrow plough in a field at Mr C Jackson's Manor House Farm. The Ivel had a two-cylinder petrol motor of eighteen horse-power, needed two men to operate when ploughing and travelled at three miles (5km) an hour. It could also run on paraffin and alcohol. The crowd was greatly impressed. The *Carlisle Patriot* reported:

'Practical farmers and agriculturists watched its operations with wonder ... an acre can be turned over with a three-furrow plough in an hour and ten minutes, doing four or five times the work of an ordinary plough with a pair of horses.'

Further, enthused the *Patriot,* the Ivel could work all day long without loss of time, such as changing over horses. It could do anything a horse could do, in fact more, drawing cultivators, sowing seed, reaping, pulling two binders or two mowing machines.

'On arrival of the motor at Dalston station on Saturday it pulled a couple of tons of bran up two steep hills to Mr Tinniswood's farm.'

Mr Tinniswood was congratulated for introducing such a modern marvel which, it was claimed, could plough eight acres (3.25ha) a day. In ordinary ploughing, pointed out the *Patriot*, that would take eight pairs of horses and eight men to do the same job.

The demonstration was a great success. Yet there was also an undercurrent of unease: talk of the need to keep people on the land, of the reduction in the number of ploughmen needed with the coming of such machines, of progress — of what would happen to the thousands of horses if everyone went in for Ivel motors?

A team of threshers at Bank End Farm, Hesket Newmarket. Threshing firms were numerous, and a particularly thriving one was that run by Henry Dowthwaite, seen here. Henry lived at Hutton Grange, Skelton, and with his son William built up a prosperous business until father and son had three threshing outfits and three road-rollers, two of them working for the county council. The Dowthwaites, on a well talked about occasion in the farming world, threshed for six and a quarter hours non-stop at Hall Rigg Farm, Plumpton, the men getting through 17½ quarters of oats an hour. The machine was filling two bags of oats every three minutes, and that was reckoned to be going some. Between them, father and son were in the threshing business for more than a hundred years.

The Famous

NOTABLE VISITORS, royalty, foreign rulers — sooner or later the famous, perhaps even the infamous, seem to turn up in the Lake District. And, once they have arrived, they are photographed visiting well-to-do friends, cutting ribbons, or just sitting back in their car eyeing the camera and being notable. Among the famous are those who were born in Lakeland, or near enough, as well as others who settled locally and then in turn have become locals themselves.

A good insight into Beatrix Potter is in this chapter; and a telling shot of the Yellow Earl with his friend the Kaiser. There is even a collection of the man of the song himself, John Peel, intent on a good blow on the horn in the only genuine photo ever taken of the huntsman, or so it is sometimes said. At least two genuine such photographs seem to exist, depending on who one listens to. One way or another, it adds to the fun.

Standing tall and decked with a line of medals, Lord Baden-Powell, founder of the Scout movement, casts a discerning eye during a parade of local Scouts in Queen's Park, Windermere, in August 1915. A proud moment for the local staff-bearer alongside: a variety of expressions from the rest of the escort.

The moment of triumph. Two strong-minded people, bailiff Tom Storey and Mrs Heelis, better known as Beatrix Potter, with their special prize-winning Herdwick at the Fell Dales Association Show at the Woolpack Inn, Eskdale, 1930.

The children's author had a side to her life that is not always known to some of her admirers. In 1913 she married an Ambleside solicitor, William Heelis, and they lived at Sawrey, a hamlet near Hawkshead on the old Lancashire side of Windermere. There, with Tom Storey's skilled help, she bred Herdwick sheep and entered them for shows, often successfully as this picture tells. She became a familiar figure for miles around at sheep sales and agricultural shows. While generally of a shy nature, she talked easily with Cumbrian farmers and many thought the world of her, though she could be rude to offcomers.

Tom Storey, like Beatrix Potter, was equally good at speaking his mind. He found the author a good person to work for. 'I wouldn't have stayed eighteen and a half years if I hadn't!' He remembered especially the day that he met her …

How did I hear of the Beatrix Potter job? … oh, I didn't know anything about it. It is a funny thing that is. Me boss knew, Neville Gregg of Town End, Troutbeck. He knew she was coming to see me because she'd made it her way to see him: got a reference, of course. She landed in on a Saturday night. Boss came into the shippon. We was finished clearing up, almost six o'clock, finishing the day's work.

He says: 'There's a lady here to see you.' I said: 'Me?' He said: 'Aye.' So I walked out, shut the door and there she was. She says: 'You'll not know me.' I says: 'No, I'm sorry I don't.'

'I'm Mrs Heelis. I've just bought Troutbeck Park, and I hear you are leaving and I want to engage you to go and manage the sheep at Troutbeck Park.'

'Well', I says, 'that's quite all right by me, if we can agree on terms.'

All she said was: 'Well, I'll double your wages, if you'll come. I'll double your wages now, whatever it is.'

Whether she knew what I was getting I don't know. I told her straight what I was getting, like. And that was that. Me boss was going to move farm, to Tebay. He didn't want a man, he wanted a boy.

There wasn't a farmer in the district as didn't know she was coming to see me. I rumbled it then, she'd been round the district getting character you know.

I went to Troutbeck Park, but before I got moved to Troutbeck in a little cottage I lambed those thousand ewes up there. After lambing time she said: 'The old man at the home farm is retiring, will you come and manage the farm for me?'

I said: 'I really prefer to be at Troutbeck Park.'

And she said: 'I think you'll benefit by it.'

So I said: 'All right, I'll give it a go.'

'Why I ask you', she said, 'I want to show Herdwick sheep.'

And I'd been used to showing Herdwick sheep with me last boss, so she'd found out likely. She said: 'I want to show Herdwick sheep and I want you to manage them for me and show them.' So I agreed. It paid me to agree. It made a good wage for it. She was a good boss that way. She was. When she engaged me I was only getting twenty-five shillings [£1.25] a week on the farm, 1926-7. She doubled it and that was a tremendous wage those days. Aye, I'd all found — milk, butter, tea. I was all right, so I came down to Sawrey on the fifteenth of June 1927. My little boy was four years old, two days before; the little girl was seven.

When all's said and done, she was a town body come into the country, if you will, and she took a fancy to farming. She didn't know a big lot about farming, you know. She relied on her men when she started farming. I could tell that when she engaged me. She had just bought Troutbeck Farm, a big sheep farm up Troutbeck, top end of Troutbeck. A thousand lambing ewes, quite a big farm, and that was why she engaged me ...

She knew nothing about sheep, you know, when all's said and done, but she learned. Anybody can learn. She was keen to learn. What she did know about farming's what she picked up after she bought these farms. She'd buy Hill Top 1906, I think it is, a stone on the wall, aye 1906, and she lived there for a while, while Castle Cottage, where she lived eventually was getting altered. Oh, she was a keen farmer and all that, but she wasn't much good on her own, if you will. After all's said and done, you couldn't expect a woman coming out of London to be a farmer, now could you?

I was with her eighteen and a half years; saw her every day, as long as she was well. I used to go across from Hill Top to Castle every morning with the milk. She'd be there every morning and opened the door.

Her sheep were bad with liver fluke when I got to 'em first, but I got that cured. She was fond of dogs. Fond of animals altogether. Guinea pigs, rabbits, ferrets. She didn't mind handling ferrets. She let 'em run up her sleeve. She'd handle anything. She'd two

Pekinese dogs and a cur dog. Rather strange, that, because when I came down I lost my dog, before I got to Sawrey.

She said: 'Will you take Lassie? She isn't working, but it may start work.' And that dog was ready for work all right. And started work right away. Made a real good dog.

Mrs Heelis — oh we got on all right, quite well, but we had some ups and downs. We didn't always agree.

Our biggest row was on the show sheep. The man as was with her before, he started showing sheep but he never won a prize with 'em, see. I thought, when I saw 'em, well it's a bit dodgy because, I thought, he never will *win a prize with this lot. So I sorted them out. And I got two out of the main flock, two ewes, and one of them was four year old and had never had a lamb, but I thought if I can get this to breed I'll go somewhere. By gum, I did — but I found out it* had *had lambs, but it had hanged them every year. Aye. It hanged 'em before anyone got to it.*

So the first year I sat up with it. I knew it was going to lamb. I could tell it was going to lamb at bedtime. So I brought it into the orchard and sat up with it. And it have done the same thing again, if I hadn't been there … just a head come, no feet. Aye, it was right I was there. Oh, it was a great lamb was that. And I tell ye, its lamb, with another lamb, won at Hawkshead that year, 1928 that would be. Aye, 1928. That was the first time she'd won anything. At Hawkshead. [Indicating the mantelpiece.] And there's *the cup she gave me the year I won all before me — in 1930.*

The row? About the sheep that I'd thrown out. She'd far too many, 200, and I cut them down to 150. I said if you want to show those sheep you must get someone else; because I won't. I told her when I came, like, that I'd get my own way, or nothing. I told her straight. That was the biggest row when she found out I'd thrown those sheep out and got one or two more in that would do the job.

She said: 'What have you thrown those out for?'

I told her I wanted nothing to do with these. I wasn't going to show those. I said they weren't show sheep. I wouldn't be seen with them in the show ring. Ooooh, she was crazy!

'Damn you!' She did swear at me, like! 'Damn you, Storey!' And she walked down the yard.

And the old man came, the boss, Mr Heelis, he was a solicitor. He came at night. 'What's going on amongst those sheep?' he said.

'Oh', I said, 'you know all about it?'

'Yes, I know all about it', he says. 'But she's not so very pleased.'

I said: 'I don't care whether she's pleased or not. It's either that, or nothing!'

Went smoother after that.

I'd heard tell when I came I wouldn't stop two years with her because she used to boss the old man and the other chaps about like toys. Oh deary, aye, she was strong-willed. She never bothered me in the end. I just used to tell her what I was going to do every day when I went with milk, that was all, but ohh …

She went to all those sheep meetings and she wouldn't go without me with her. I was the stooge, if you will. If she wanted to answer a question, she asked me what it was. At sheep sales, she didn't do any buying. I did the buying. I used to pick out what sheep we wanted and show her them. 'If you're satisfied', she'd say, 'I'm satisfied.' Well I had to buy them. There was no expense spared, mind. She wanted the best. Aye.

A cup winner — 1930, champion female — Herdwick. Ennerdale, Loweswater, Eskdale — those three shows, she'd only put those three shows in because, she used to say, they were the only Herdwick shows there was. But still they always used to go to the other shows as well! At the end of that season I was surprised when she came at Christmas and presented me with that cup. I thought, well, that is a nice gesture, anyway, and it is solid silver. That year, though, I did it more than once, I went to every show there was in Westmorland and Cumberland. There was Bowness — I didn't count that — Hawkshead, Keswick, Wigton, Loweswater, Ennerdale, Eskdale and Gosforth and I was never beaten that year. 1930. In the end they were a grand lot of sheep.

Oh, I grew to like her ... it was a bit dicey at first. Aye, it was that! I had a cottage ready to go back to, I tell ye, when I saw what she was like, really. Well, I thought, I'll pin her down or I'll leave. But it was showing sheep that did it, finished her off in the end, like. Aye, she found out she was bossed. I respected her for that.

Oh, she was a character, there's no doubt about that. The way she dressed for a start. You never saw her really dressed up. In one of these old herringbone tweed skirts down to the ankles, always. Never any different, and her clogs on. When she was president of the Sheep Breeders' Association she went in her clogs and I went with her, to Cockermouth, to t' general meeting. She went to shows in her clogs. At Hill Top, yon big picture of her, that's the year she was president at Keswick Show. She was in her clogs that day, course you can't see her clogs. She went to every show. Mr Heelis used to take her. She was supposed to be shy, but she'd talk days and days with the old fell farmers, you know. They thought the world of her, although they were getting beat!

The funniest thing ever happened was at Keswick Show. I never forgot that. Shouldn't tell mebbe against her. But oh, we'd finished showing. I won the ewe, two-sheer shearing, and lambs, and only got second prize for next ewe, and we'd finished and they were all back in their pens, and the man as had retired was there at the show and she had cottoned on to him and she was walking round with him. I was with a local lad. She'd got to the fence to show her show sheep. I was just across.

She pointed and said: 'Storey! Which is the short-necked ewe?' She was pointing at the sheep.

I said: 'Neither of them.' They were Billy Rigg's. Another farmer's altogether. I was really embarrassed. I didn't know what to say.

We had a bit of a barney another time. I forget what it was about. She went across to my wife after. A little bad-tempered devil, she called me. Wife used to laugh. My wife when I was getting a bit natterly would say: 'You little bad-tempered devil.' Aye!

If you wanted anything to improve the farm she would pay. Such as lime, or anything like that, to make things grow. Yes, she was all right that way. The only thing

Beatrix pauses in among the sheep pens at the Woolpack Show in Eskdale, 1933.

I had against her was she was slow in getting forrard with implements. Everybody else was using implements before we got any. She liked the old-fashioned way. Hard work; hands. Aye. Scalers, turners, hay turners. We had horses then. But I will say, this, we were the first to have a tractor round here. With a bailer. We were forced to plough those days. So much ploughing every two or three years, and self-binders. At haytime we were raking by hand while other folk had implements. But she found out it was better to have implements in the end; faster on.

A good business woman ... oh yes. Course any business, real *business, he [Mr Heelis] did for her.*

Shorthorn cattle ... she had a niece very keen on Shorthorns who called and used to come every year to book them down, their offspring and so forth. We used to give them names, just to pacify Mrs Heelis really ... Nancy was a favourite, a white cow. A Shorthorn. There was Julie, Janet, and Muriel. She didn't insist, but we knew she liked them.

She only judged at one show as I remember, that was Lowick. Let's see, now, about 1935-6. I remember I had to go with her. There were two on us. She said: 'If I want any advice, Tom, you be at the ringside.' There were two judges. The other old man was a good hand, like, he kept things straight. Yes, she was little bit nervous.

Aeroplanes ... she didn't like those flying over. She'd defend horses, for one thing. Working with a horse in the hayfield she was frightened they might bolt.

She used to go across the lake every Sunday to her mother's for lunch, at Lindeth Howe, behind the hill going to Crook, a fair-sized house. She often went to Troutbeck Church to worship.

Things have changed a bit ... today she'd have gone crazy. Didn't like folk about, you know. Cars, an that ... though I guess she was expecting it, because the wife always said: 'She's expecting this place to open after her day, in memory.' I said: 'Why?' 'The stuff she's bringing into it, the old oak and such like.'

She used to write in there, you know. I bet she was starved to death many a time. Sitting in there in cold. A cold house, no fire on. Writing. Books, you know. Nice and quiet, no servants up there. She could hear every word we said in the house next door and we didn't know she was in there. She went to Hill Top to write her tales when living at Castle Cottage.

She wasn't a hard person to work for. As long as she knew you were working, and she knew you were a worker, she didn't bother you. I'll give her her due there.

That green pasture across the road. That was her favourite place, reet at t' top of the hill, the highest point on that pasture. She sat out. There's a stone there, a flat stone there she used to sit on. Aye, the stone's still there. Sat drawing and writing, in the summer. She used to go across the meadow. She had a stile put over the wire fence to make it easy. The stile was taken down when the new museum started.

Aye, she was a character and I reckon I was lucky to know her. Well I was. Nothing to see her going over that hill over there with a basket on her arm going shopping in Hawkshead, a sack round her shoulder, a cake sack, cake used to come in 'em, keep the rain out.

Married: Beatrix and William, a portrait taken in London. The wedding was on the 15th October 1913, at St Mary Abbot's Parish Church, Kensington, he a gentle-mannered Lakeland solicitor with a wry sense of humour, she a storyteller of considerable ability and charm. With this settled and happy marriage, Mrs Beatrix Heelis turned to a new and absorbing life as a housewife and farmer. She became a generous supporter of the National Trust, helping with gifts of property and money in her lifetime, and with a considerable bequest of land and property on her death. Shy as a child, she remained a private-natured person all her life.

She met a tramp top of the hill there at Sawrey. A pedlar, if you will. He was carrying his basket as well and it was raining and teeming down. And the old chap said: 'Ehh, it's a bad day for the likes of thee and me, missis!' He thought she was a pedlar an' all. She telled that story herself, you know. That suited her. She agreed with him. Didn't tell him any different. She would take a joke like that all right.

But err, she could be funny. We got on all right, like, but I don't doubt if I'd knuckled under it would have bin different.

She med a fortune with writing children's stories and children's books … yet she didn't like children, it's no good saying different. She didn't care for children, you know. They were frightened to death, children in the village; they were frightened to death of her. Well, if made any noise … she couldn't bear them to make any noise. Ohh, she would tell them off if they were playing in the village and making a noise. That didn't do. Well, what can you expect, children, they always make bit of a row, don't they? 'Keep quiet! Don't make so much noise!' They went in, and some of 'em ran home, you know.

Every year just for showing sheep and doing well with 'em I got a real good cheque off her at Christmas. Yes. She gave the rest something, too. But mine was a cheque. She gave me a book, The Fairy Caravan. *One of the first twelve, printed in America. She brought them to England. 'For Tom Storey from the author, Beatrix Heelis, in remembrance of Queenie, Oct 26, 1929.' One of our favourite show sheep.*

There was nothing snobbish about her. A bonny woman up to the last. I can picture her the last night I saw her, the night before she died. A quiet person. Mr Heelis came in one day. We'd just finished dinner. He handed me the box and said: 'You know what to do with these, Storey.'

I said: 'What is it?' 'Cause I just didn't know.

He said: 'Mrs Heelis's ashes'.

'Oh', I said, 'yes, I know where they have to go.' Because she'd told me what to do.

I felt a bit queer at first, you know. That was biggest shock when she asked me if I would scatter them for her. Course I had to swear to her I would tell nobody. I said yes, I'd scatter them.

Time and again the name of a remarkable man occurs in Lakeland life, that of Canon Hardwicke Rawnsley. Lively, often controversial, he was one of the great protectors of the Lake District, passionate in his love of nature and constantly inspired by the beauty of the lake counties and their wild fells.

The canon, who was the vicar at Wray for a time, and then for thirty-four years at Crosthwaite, Keswick, had tremendous energy and enthusiasm — and a fiery temper. He led many campaigns against threatened encroachments on the natural beauty of the district and often championed local inhabitants, protecting their wellbeing. In 1883 he was instrumental in founding the Lake District Defence Society, which beat off a proposed railway scheme into Ennerdale; and in 1895, with Octavia Hill and Sir Robert Hunter, he helped to found the National Trust and was its honorary secretary until his death in 1920.

The canon wrote thirty-seven books about Lakeland life and had a gift for composing appropriate verses on any occasion, often on the spur of the moment. His wit was well known, often drawing on reliable sources for his inspiration. As he pointed out, the Cockermouth, Keswick and Penrith Railway, the CKP, was mentioned in the first chapter of Genesis (verse 25): 'And God made everything that creepeth on earth.' To be fair, the line did include some dramatic gradients.

Rawnsley travelled widely, and spoke on many causes — footpaths, education, litter, housing for refugees. He plunged into battle impulsively, rightly or wrongly, but enthusiastically. His influence extended into many areas of national and local life. Through him and others, much of the National Trust's early properties in Lakeland and elsewhere were acquired.

No doubt that he made some enemies; to some he was a fiery busybody, but to the majority he was a large-hearted man who cared passionately for his flock.

The canon was buried in Crosthwaite churchyard, as he had wished. And in September 1922, Hardwicke's friends and many admirers whom he had inspired honoured his memory by presenting Lords Island, Friars Crag and a part of the shore of Derwentwater to the National Trust.

Straight backed and seemingly a little aloof, the poet laureate Alfred Lord Tennyson sits with the Howard family as their guest during a visit to Naworth Castle, Brampton, about 1875. In the centre of the long covered garden seat is the slight figure of Rosalind, countess of Carlisle, wife of the ninth earl and renowned for her autocratic manner. Rosalind ran the Naworth Estate, and threw herself into the temperance movement and women's suffrage. On the right is the Hon Charles Howard MP, father of the ninth earl, with Lady Mary Howard on his knee.

Tennyson appeared to the Howards as somewhat touchy and sensitive, and needing an audience when he spoke. Rosalind, whose own reputation was that of a forthright, purposeful person, said that at times she had found the poet vain, pompous and boorish, but still good to talk to and friendly. She sang a number of Tennyson's songs, but found some of his poetry 'rather weary'. Tennyson probably had an opinion about the countess.

Bearded philosopher, art critic and social reformer, Professor John Ruskin and Sir Henry Acland, Bart, are caught deep in discussion. Ruskin had a life-long love of the Lakes but he did not settle in the district for many years. Then, in 1871, when he was fifty-three, he bought Brantwood on the eastern side of Coniston Water. It was a large cottage at the time, with a striking view across the lake to Coniston Old Man. He bought it without seeing it, and once in residence he gradually converted the property and its gardens into a fine house, a kind of poet's paradise where he spent the rest of his life.

The writer A H Griffin wrote warmly about 'this extraordinarily gifted man', a kindly genius whose collected works amounted to some thirty-five volumes, and who was once described as the greatest of the Lakes celebrities, including Wordsworth. A superb painter of prose and poetry.

While to local people he was kindly and friendly, Ruskin strongly opposed industrial civilisation, opposed railways, and especially the idea that one day Lakeland might be overrun by hoards of tourists.

For many years he worked on his books, tended the gardens and involved himself in local affairs. He strongly argued for social and economic planning.

In the final stages of his life, he experienced attacks of mental illness and within days of his eighty-first birthday he died, in 1900, from influenza. There was talk of a grave and national homage in Westminster Abbey, but Ruskin's wish had been to be buried in Coniston churchyard, and that is what happened. To many he was known as the Professor, and there are still admirers from all parts of the world who call in on his lovely home to catch a little of the ambience of a remarkable man.

Boy in a white sailor suit. The photographer little knew as he took this picture back in 1919 that this Cumberland lad was destined to become one of Lakeland's finest poets.

Norman Nicholson was about five years old as he sat in Hargreave's studio in Dalton in Furness with this bowl and clay pipe. The pose was a popular one, with the photographers if not with the sitters, and was prompted by the portrait *Bubbles* by Sir John Millais, which became famous as a Pears Soap advertisement.

Norman, in his engaging autobiography *Wednesday Early Closing*, recalls that the basin in his lap was cold against his legs and he launched a howl of protest. Hastily a piece of newspaper was put between the bowl and his legs, and soon he was 'gazing upwards with hypnotised attention' at a huge soap bubble which, in fact, was not there for it was added in afterwards by the photographer. 'Yet to my mother, that bubble was perhaps more real than anything else in the picture ...'

Norman, born in Millom, wrote poetry throughout much of his life, as well as plays and Lakeland topographical books. Many regard him as the best Cumbrian poet since Wordsworth.

Knowing eyes, and an appealing glint of humour. Arthur Ransome, the master storyteller who captured the hearts of thousands of children with his books, knew Lakeland as well as anyone. As a child he enjoyed many lake country holidays, especially at Nibthwaite on Coniston Water, which he grew to love and where so often he observed his secret rite of dipping a hand into the water as a kind of greeting to the lake, and a sure way of knowing he had returned. Even in his later years he performed the little act, laughing a little at himself for doing so.

As a young man he lived in Chelsea, leading a Bohemian life as a struggling writer, writing books of literary criticism and on story telling. In 1913 he went to Russia to learn the language and to study the folklore. During the First World War he became a war correspondent from the Russian front for the *Daily News* and later special correspondent of the *Manchester Guardian*, and graphically reported the Russian Revolution which he saw at first hand in 1917.

He met his future wife, Evgenia, then working as Trotsky's secretary, and eventually they moved to Lakeland, where between 1930 and 1945 Ransome wrote his famous *Swallows and Amazons* series of books. They had a number of homes in the lake country, including Lowick Hall, near the River Crake — boats and fishing were always among Ransome's great delights — and at Hill Top, Haverthwaite, near Newby Bridge.

In 1923, before the *Swallows and Amazons* adventures, Ransome wrote *Racundra's First Cruise*, a book based on a ketch he had built at the Baltic port of Riga. In later years *Racundra* was to have numerous owners. During the 1960s it was found in a ramshackled condition in southern Spain, and was bought by an adopted uncle of mine who offered me the chance to live on board at Gibraltar, which I did for a glorious sailing summer.

The face in the crowd. Hugh Walpole, hatless, novelist, an urban man who found 'a little paradise' on Cat Bells. As a child he spent holidays near Gosforth, but not until he was almost forty did he return to the Lake District to settle. He arrived on a week's holiday at Troutbeck and that visit changed his whole life, for he decided to live at Brackenburn in Borrowdale.

He wrote in a study built above his garage, a beloved den looking out across Derwentwater, though in fact he was often absent, seldom home longer than five weeks at a time in the seventeen years he owned the house. He was greatly liked by many Cumbrians and made many friends.

He wrote at a tremendous pace, sometimes more than a thousand words an hour, and hardly corrected a word. Apart from his four Herries novels and *A Prayer for My Son*, centred on Keswick, he wrote little about the Lake District, though he wrote some sixty books. Even so, his reputation as a Lakeland writer is considerable. The Herries quartet, *Rogue Herries, Judith Paris, The Fortress* and *Vanessa,* proved to be a great success and are still widely read.

A certain hotel at Bowness, Windermere, has often been a popular choice with foreign guests when visiting Lakeland. Numerous members of the royal family have stayed there, as well as Sir Henry Segrave, Kaiser Wilhelm II, the emperor of Germany, and many others. In flowing robes, and a generous smile, this was the day the Sultan of Zanzibar arrived.

A sprig of white heather in his lapel, the duke of Windsor pauses outside the Old England Hotel, Bowness, for a word with Lord Lonsdale and R Bownass during a motor tour of Lakeland in the summer of 1927. The duke, who arrived at Bowness Bay by boat, was greeted by a fleet of fast motorboats which surged into the bay, where for a time the duke took the controls of a launch and had a spin round Belle Isle.

The famous huntsman and farmer John Peel of Caldbeck had just one photograph taken of him, it is said, though if that is true then which is the real one is often a matter of argument. Claims have been made about the two shown here — that both are of Peel, though possibly one of them is really one of the huntsman's sons. Whatever the case, there are also plenty of drawings and paintings of the famous man from which to choose.

The facts about Peel vary from book to book, though the number thirteen seems to have been recurring. He was born at Greenrigg, a simple house in Caldbeck village (others say he was born at Park End Farm, not a long way off, and was taken to Greenrigg when a few days old). His date of birth was the 13th November 1776 (1777 says another source); he was one of a family of thirteen children; his own children numbered thirteen, seven sons and six daughters; he weighed about thirteen stone, and he died on the 13th November 1854 (or ten years later, in 1864, according to a

The real John Peel?

Another John Peel — or was this one of his sons?

widely sold postcard). All the surmise aside, what is certain is that he is buried at Caldbeck.

Peel's reputation as a huntsman was deserved. He was a superb if inelegant horseman, a remarkable man in some ways. On one occasion he is said to have caught a hare by bending down in the saddle and seizing it mid-jump. He was a heavy drinker, rough spoken with a loud voice. He stood more than six feet (2m) in height, and had piercing blue eyes. According to his contemporaries, hunting came before money, job, wife or children. He rode with his knees high, feet in a short stirrup, and on a crossbred pony of no more than 14.3 hands (1.45m).

John Peel's steed, a roan Galloway called Dunny, followed him about like a dog once the huntsman had dismounted. Whatever else is said about the uneducated, hard-riding man, apparently both hounds and horse would go anywhere with him, and their affection was returned.

The many faces of John Peel.

In his coat so grey — still occasionally mistakenly called gay — Peel hunted across Cumberland, and some of the foxes he chased went as far as sixty miles (95km) before being caught. His coat would likely have been made from wool from the local Herdwick sheep, spun and woven in the village, and amazingly durable.

Peel was made famous by the song *D'ye ken John Peel?*, written by John Woodcock Graves, owner of a woollen mill in Caldbeck. The original tune was a somewhat uninspiring 'Bonnie Annie', but William Metcalfe, Carlisle Cathedral organist, liked the words and gave it its present world-famous setting. As Graves said: 'By jove, Peel, you'll be sung when we're both run to earth.' That is certainly true.

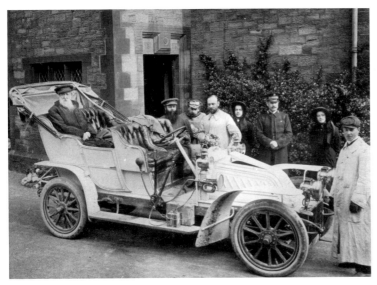

General Booth, the founder of the Salvation Army, sits back in his white car outside St George's Vicarage, Millom, with members of his support team standing around. It is August 1905, and the white-bearded general is on a 2,000 mile (3,000km) tour of the North of England with six motor cars full of officers on a powerful recruiting campaign. Already they have held meetings in Carnforth, Kendal and Ulverston, and after an overnight stay in Millom the general's eye-catching cavalcade is ready to drive on to Whitehaven, Workington and Maryport. The general, at seventy-six, was, according to a local newspaper, 'bearing up well'.

A fine display of wealthy hats and bristly moustaches. It is October 1907, and sitting in the centre is Princess Louise of Schleswig-Holstein on the steps of Levens Hall, long the home of the Bagot family. The princess was fond of historic houses, and Levens, a few miles south of Kendal, was one she greatly enjoyed, for part of it dates from 1188, with its renowned topiary gardens laid out by Beaumont, who also laid out Hampton Court grounds for James II. In the line-up, from the left: rear, Major Noble, Captain Roebuck, Mr Gordon Wordsworth; middle, Miss Hawkes, the princess, Mrs Bagot; front, Miss Bagot, Captain Bagot and Mrs Noble.

Hugh Lowther, the fifth earl of Lonsdale, or Lordy as he was affectionately called, kept up an amazing scale of living. His estate at its peak was said to embrace the lakes of Windermere, Grasmere and Haweswater, much of the town of Whitehaven, rich extensive coalfields in West Cumberland, iron mines and much else, including near Penrith his ancestral Lowther Castle.

Born in London in 1857, Hugh was a tall, high-spirited man, direct and generous, quick-tempered sometimes if his orders were not carried out precisely, but quick to recover his good humour. He was highly inventive, a perfectionist with a quick, original mind. His passions were many, and the greatest of these was sport — hunting, boxing, wrestling, swimming, yachting, shooting, racing. He loved them all.

Strong among his attributes was a deep instinct for fair play. It won him the admiration of thousands of people, and a reputation at home and abroad as England's greatest sportsman. Even the earl's indiscretions, his support for unpopular causes, his involvement with beautiful women, seemed to increase rather than diminish his popularity with the public.

Lordy had sandy-coloured hair. It was this that some claim gave rise to his Yellow Earl nickname, though in fact yellow had been the family colour before his day and

Hugh Cecil Lowther, the controversial fifth earl of Lonsdale, sits astride his dappled horse and contemplates his vast Cumbrian estate. His spending power was estimated at some £4,000 a week, though how to spend it did not seem to present a problem.

Lowther Castle, near Penrith. It had a staff of at least fifty. There were 365 rooms, and guests frequently became lost in its halls and corridors.

had been adopted locally by the Conservatives — rather than the customary blue — perhaps because the Lonsdales had much political influence. The earl applied yellow wherever it could be used effectively, and one of the grand sights was his fleet of horse-drawn carriages passing through the countryside. They were magnificent carriages in canary yellow with black wheels, and Lordy's coronet on the doors; immaculate chestnut horses were ridden by postillions in yellow jackets, white breeches and black caps and boots, and each carried a silver-mounted whip. The cavalcade was greatly admired and so it should have been, for the carriages allegedly had a minimum of eighteen coats of paint.

Lordy inherited Lowther Castle with an agricultural estate of more than 50,000 acres (2,000ha), plus 50,000 acres of common land, including sporting and mineral rights. The castle was a giant of its kind, with 365 rooms and a small army of servants geared to running it smoothly. Guests frequently became lost in its halls and corridors when looking for their bedrooms.

Whenever the earl was in residence — he spent much of his time in the south — a staff of at least fifty sat down to meals. Including house guests, the number of people to feed four times a day sometimes rose to more than a hundred and the tempo below stairs occasionally bordered on frenzy. But Lordy had it well organised. Every week a game cart was sent to Whitehaven for fresh fish. Meat came from London and was collected off the train; it never came from Penrith, and no one but the earl seemed to know why. The castle cellars were large, rack after rack of wine, vats of gin and whisky, and barrels of beer.

The household staff were directed by the earl rather on army lines. There was a strict protocol: the head butler, the under butler, first footman, second footman and third footman, the housekeeper and her seven housemaids — fifty staff at least and, centre stage, the figure of the cook, who not only ruled her own private unit of three kitchen maids, two stillroom maids, three scullery maids and an unknown number of

The German army manoeuvres in 1904. In spiked helmet, Kaiser Wilhelm II, emperor of Germany, and Hugh Lowther, fifth earl of Lonsdale, are caught in discussion. The emperor had appointed Lordy to an honorary position on his staff. Their friendship caused some sharp criticism in Britain.

daily helps, but also enjoyed the privilege of eating her breakfast, cooked by the first kitchen maid, in her own sitting room.

Ruled by the clock, geared to meal times, Lowther represented an amazing scale of living. Daily some thirty or so stable hands polished the carriages and groomed the horses. And daily the Lowther coat of arms was remade in colours on sand freshly laid in the yard, until destroyed during inspection by Lordy's romping labradors, bred as close to yellow as possible.

The gardens at Lowther became famous. Lordy devised a mile (1.5km) long border of trees and shrubs, and an ornamental lake. There were miles of yew hedges, a large alpine garden, and a Japanese garden with bronze birds, scarlet bridges and stone shrines. On hearing that the neighbouring Greystoke Castle had a park larger than his own, Lordy ordered that the fences of twenty adjacent farms should be flattened. Thus Lowther Park grew to 4,000 acres (1,600ha) of open countryside, said to be the biggest in Britain.

To Lowther Castle came many visitors, and none more controversial than Kaiser Wilhelm II, Queen Victoria's grandson. Lordy's friendship with the German emperor sparked considerable criticism among politicians, but Lordy ignored them. He liked Wilhelm, who visited him as his guest on two occasions, in 1898 and 1902. Everything

Hugh lords it in a ninety horse-power Napier with chauffeur Tony Hirsch, who was persuaded to quit his job in Germany and work for the Yellow Earl at Lowther Castle. Another German, Johann William Kieser, who had been chauffeuring for the German emperor, Kaiser Wilhelm II, at the German Army manoeuvres in 1904, had done likewise, and worked as head chauffeur to Lordy at Lowther for several years.

was done to make the emperor's stay pleasant. He took a trip on Ullswater in the *Raven*, then a steam vessel; he went on tourist jaunts, with dinner at the Old England in Bowness, and on one occasion Lordy staged a rabbit shoot for him. The kaiser had a crippled arm and did not find shooting easy, so Lordy made sure all went smoothly by ordering the capture of hundreds of rabbits. These were taken to a wood and, when the emperor was in position, they were released. Hundreds of rabbits rushed at the kaiser and in a frantic shooting session he shot sixty-seven in half an hour.

Lordy was the guest of Wilhelm at the annual German army manoeuvres on the Continent, and during his 1904 visit he was driven around in a Mercedes car. The vehicle had been lent to the kaiser by the Daimler motor works and he placed it at the disposal of Lordy, who was greatly impressed by its performance. The outcome was that Wilhelm presented the car to Lordy as a gift.

Daimler had done more than provide the vehicle, they had also supplied one of their own enthusiastic engineers as a chauffeur, twenty year old Johann Wilhelm Kieser. Lordy, who could not drive, liked Mr Kieser and persuaded him to come to England to Lowther at £15 a month as head chauffeur-mechanic.

Before leaving Germany, Lordy discovered that the bright metalwork on his car was only silver plated and not real silver as he had supposed. The earl gave instructions for his new employee to return with the car to the factory and have the matter put right, and so the car was dismantled and eventually silver fittings replaced the plating, just as on the Lonsdale carriages.

The earl, while never having the same faith in cars as he had in horses, nevertheless in the years up to the First World War owned at least fourteen private vehicles, mostly Napiers. Extra chauffeurs were engaged — including a fellow countryman to Mr Kieser, Tony Hirsch — and they were kitted out with brown double-breasted jackets, matching breeches and gaiters, buttons and badges of silver, and collar facings in Lonsdale yellow.

In 1911, Lordy became the first president of the Automobile Association, and down the years it has been said that he allowed the AA to adopt his personal colour as their own, though the association in fact had been using yellow before 1911, mainly for road signs.

The First World War ended Lordy's friendship with Wilhelm, and the earl energetically set about promoting the war against Germany. Once the conflict had ended, the two men exchanged Christmas greetings.

Lordy's chauffeur Johann Kieser loyally served the earl for seven years, married and raised a family, and then in 1911, with his employer's blessing, took over the Whitelock Brothers cycle firm in Penrith, where he was well liked and ran his own successful motor business. Mr Kieser became naturalised in 1913 and served with the British Army during the First World War, an ironic twist for he did so knowing that his brother was in the German Army. Years later, J W Kieser's business was taken over by Dias and Co of Carlisle.

For a time it seemed that nothing would stop Lordy's lifestyle, but in the end the upkeep of the castle proved too costly and the trustees got their way. In 1936 they forced him to leave Lowther in a move to bring about economies. He died in Barleythorpe in Rutland in 1944. As for the castle, eventually the contents were sold to help pay off considerable debts and only a shell was left. The extravagance and splendour that was Lordy passed away. In the eyes of some he squandered a fortune but, if so, he had done so magnificently.

Trundlers and Trotters

A<small>T TIMES IT IS</small> hard to appreciate the enormous change that has taken place in travel, from the slower, long-established rhythms of the past to the apparent headlong rush of the present. Scarcely a hundred years or so ago, many families in Lakeland's rural communities clung much closer to their homesteads than we do. If they did go anywhere special, they travelled by horse and cart, or by cycle, or a train if a station were handy, but mostly they walked …

Walked the sheep and cattle to the auctions. Walked to school. Walked to church. Walked into town to have a tooth pulled (not always with the benefit of anaesthetic) and then walked home nursing their jaw; walked across the fells when courting a girl in the next valley. And every week the walk to market, a wicker basket loaded with butter covered in muslin over one arm, a basket of eggs over the other, to sell at a street stall and then home again, with the groceries, perhaps twelve miles (19km) there and back in the day.

Horses, of course, made life easier. For centuries the horse was king. Ploughing, hauling timber, pulling carts; something like 1,000 horses in Keswick in 1910, half of them in the tourist industry; in all Cumberland and Westmorland in 1919 about 34,000, most of them in farming. Today, in comparison, almost none, obliterated by motor vehicles — buses, cars, lorries, but on farms mainly by the arrival of tractors; it happened seemingly quite quickly.

Bicycles likewise proved a great boon. Thousands took to cycling, especially in the 1890s, and dismally many coachmen saw bicycles as a threat to their livelihood. To that worry, motor cars were soon added.

Another big change came with the arrival of the railways. The lines had encircled the Cumbrian mountains back in the thrusting Victorian times, carrying everything from iron ore to slate, but also altering the centuries-old patterns of droving. It was quicker to transport cattle and sheep to market by train than to walk them. The railways, too, opened the way to huge numbers of tourists. A mid-Victorian tourist boom resulted. And others followed.

On the lakes, boats played their part, both in tourism and commercially. The Windermere ferry goes back a long way, some 600 years or more; an important link between Lancashire and Westmorland, and a good way to avoid a long haul round England's longest lake, ten and a half miles (17km).

But it is to motor cars we should look the hardest. Few were around in Lakeland at the start of the last century. A doctor might own one for his rounds, or a well-to-do landowner might have one, though it was not long before this initial trickle became a flood. In 1900 in all Britain there were an estimated 800 motor vehicles on the roads; by the First World War there were more than 132,000. Compare that with today, when at peak times in the summer in Cumbria, taking an average on just a stretch of the A66 between Penrith and Keswick, a motor vehicle passes every five seconds, or more than 700 an hour. To put it another way, someone somewhere has worryingly worked out that, thanks to the modern roads, an estimated 7,000,000 people could now arrive by car in Lakeland within three and a half hours of setting out, if they chose to do so. One has only to see a hundred motor vehicles in a temper-hot traffic jam at the top of Wrynose Pass on a busy summer's day, drivers literally out in the road in a punch-up (it has been witnessed), and it is easy to sense that it might be more tranquil at home.

Motor vehicles have done something else: they have helped families to uproot themselves from the community easily, and have made possible a new lifestyle, to commute daily from farms and converted barn houses to town and city jobs, and be home again in the dales by nightfall. So while many still live within the folds of Cumbria, the number of people working the land is greatly reduced. At many a stead just a farmer, his wife and a tractor — that's how it seems nowadays. The sons have driven off elsewhere to earn a living.

The words are few and carved on a slab of Lakeland stone:

'Fallen from his fellow's side
The steed beneath is lying,
In harness here he died,
His only fault was dying.

WB'

The traffic races past and few people pause to read the little plaque that was set in a wall near Thirlmere, for it is a dangerous narrow section of the Ambleside–Keswick road and an unwise place to stop. Many a man and many a woman has wept tears when their horse has died. Thousands were once at work on the farms; thousands more were on the roads in transport. Once motor cars began to take over, whole armies of horses went to the knacker's, and though everything became faster and more efficient, a bit of the heart went out of things as the horse lost its place. 'More faithful to me, my horse, than I to myself.' That was what they used to say.

Sixty horses at work at Langton Field Farm, Appleby — a *boon ploughing day* on a grand scale.

Boon days were often arranged when a farmer took on a new farm or changed farms. On this occasion, in 1913-14, the Threlkeld family left Langton Field and the Ewin family took over. Neighbours sent men and teams of horses, and gave the newcomers a day's work to help them get a good start. This practical gesture also helped to make the newcomers feel welcome.

In some places, the first teams to arrive on boon days received a bow of ribbon for man and horses to wear. The day's work might include sowing and rolling, and even leaving a cartload of muck for the land. Middens long ago were regarded as a valuable asset, and at times were mentioned in wills and even bequeathed to a relative or friend.

During boon ploughing day, the women likewise never stopped work, preparing food and taking it to the workmen. When the ploughing was over, a *merry neet* would follow, perhaps in a barn or the farm kitchen, with a generous spread, and games of cards for the old, and dancing to fiddle and accordion music for the young. This generous boon custom continued until well into the last century.

On occasions the ploughings have gone awry. In the excitement of horse teams arriving, over-eager ploughmen have been known to start work on the wrong field, quickly halted once the error was noticed, but leaving the job of levelling off unwanted furrows to the new family.

Jim Brown and his travelling stallion, Gallant Print, at Whitrigg Moor, Kirkbride, 1927. 'Gallant Print is a horse rare to be with, a sure foal getter — and his gets are an eye opener.' So said Mr Brown's cheerfully outspoken schedule extolling the stallion's ability to serve the waiting mares of North Cumberland. And there is no doubt that Gallant Print was looking fit, standing well and, indeed, a very beautiful horse.

The usual term for a serving stallion was an entire — meaning that it had all its working parts. Each year many scores of entires travelled the roads from farm to farm, sometimes alternating the routes from one week to the next so as to arrive when the mares needed them. In 1927 it cost £1 to have a mare served by Gallant Print, paid at the end of the season, plus £3, unless a mare proved not to be in foal.

Jim Brown made no bones about Gallant Print's qualities:

'He stands 17 hands with weight and substance, great limbs and a wide good wearing foot, and moves to perfection at both ends. He is in fact a lorry horse and it takes weight to shift weight and command the price in the sale ring.'

In short, Gallant Print was a good bet for breeding a commercial horse. And so, too, apparently were his hired hands. Jim Brown's newspaper adverts claimed that not only were the horses 'the very best' but 'so are the lads with them'. Mr Brown's publicity extended to a burst of doggerel:

> 'Here's health and success to the Horse Gallant Print,
> He has size, weight and substance and new from the Mint,
> His type, with his breeding, is bad to excel,
> with great feet and legs and as sound as a bell.
> His gets are eye-openers when they come to the sales,
> And his first crop of foals were nearly all males,
> In conclusion take notice and quietly take hint,
> And to benefit yourselves patronize Gallant Print.'

The arrival of an entire at a farm to serve the mares at times created a bit of a stir among the hands. Old-timer Robert W recalls in a letter the effect it had on the watching women servants:

'Langholm, Thurs

Dear Mr Fellman,

Your letter in *Cumberland News* brought back some of my more sinful school days in Langholm. At that time (1912–13) a man and stallion travelled the district and serviced mares on the farms. A mate and I took truant off school to see the servicing on a few of the farms. It generally took place in the farmyard where the servant girls were often present.

A few years ago I and some friends were having a drink and chat of the good old days when the travelling "stallion" was mentioned and one of the ladies had witnessed a service on the farm where she was employed etc. She told us her "Fanny" twittered for a week after seeing the scene.

She also knew the man who was in charge of the stallion, and that he fathered more illigitimate children on his rounds, as the stallion did foals.

Yours sincerely,
Robt. W.'

Farmer George Mason, of Windy Hall, Rusland Valley, worked with horses all his life. He missed them more than he could say …

Horses is like people: different characters. Some was a lot of work. Stupid and all kinds of things. Some could kick. I got kicked in face once, just like that. Used to groom 'em late at night after a day in t' fields. Three hours grooming three horses; got plastered in mud. They come to expect being groomed. Some objected, like people. Some lasted only a few years, some went lame quick. Some lasted seven or eight years. Ten some.

A lot of old horses went to the knackers at the finish. Folk had made their living out of 'em. Some hands thought a lot on 'em. There's been a lot of tears on farms when horses was sold. I had one, Sam. He just dropped down dead. A heart attack. I wept a bucket, and I was gone forty.

It was a bad feeling when a horse died. You got attached to 'em. A lot were intelligent; they understood your mood when they got to know you. I knew their mood too. You could see when they weren't right side out. I misses 'em more than I can say. There's a few does. They go back a long way does horses.

The man walks, the woman rides, July 1910. One-horse-power mowing is under way during haytime at Larches Farm, Torver, Coniston. Farmer's daughter May Smith is wearing a *clootie bonnet*, a practical piece of headgear which shades the eyes and has a generous flap to protect the back of the neck against the sun. Lending a hand is Jack Gregg, a quarryman from Torver. In the background is a stretch of the now-vanished railway line to Coniston, though its course can still be determined easily enough. It was opened in 1859 mainly for carrying copper ore, and was developed by Furness Railway as a tourist route. The line lasted until 1962.

Harnessing up for a day's work.

Hauling timber, Rusland Valley, c1909. Much of Rusland's timber ended at the woodyard at Greenodd where ships were once built.

The timber men, if they were often tough in their dealings with other people, in general were kind enough to their beasts, working long into the evening, after the day's work was over, to ensure their horses were brushed down, watered and fed before they settled to their own meal. Getting their horses reshod was often another evening task. Down-valley at Oxen Park smithy, queues of horses formed in the gloom as late as ten or eleven o'clock at night, awaiting their turn.

The horses often worked in teams and timber hauling was considered to be one of the hardest of all their jobs. When tractors took over, many a timber man lamented that whereas a horse dragged a chained trunk out of the woods with no damage to other trees around it, picking its way with sure feet, the tractors, though faster, chewed destructively at anything that got in the way. Delivering timber undamaged was a matter of pride to the timber men, whose rough language often shielded considerable affection for their hard-working beasts.

One horse and a hefty load ready for moving off. The tripod in the hands of experienced woodmen worked well and made otherwise difficult loading jobs possible. Perhaps one should feel a bit sorry for the horse.

Timber team at Satterthwaite village, High Furness.

The 30th June 1921 was a sad day, the dispersal sale of a Lakeland legend. Forty-one horses have made their last run for Riggs. From the *Westmorland Gazette*, 25th June 1921.

A Riggs stagecoach halts in Keswick with a full load of passengers. Richard Rigg, of the Windermere Hotel, ran one of Lakeland's best-known stagecoach firms and had some 200 horses at work at the peak of the tourist season.

The coachmen wore a smart box hat and a scarlet coat, and were known far and wide as Robin Redbreasts. Many a Lakeland youngster longed to join this elite band, and drive the eye-catching black and yellow coaches. On the off-chance, some went to the Riggs stables to offer help. Every buckle had to be polished, the harnesses cleaned, the stables left tidy. The lads helped with it all, and lived in hope.

But the stagecoach trade did not last. At one point bicycles had been feared by the coachmen as a major threat to their liveli-hood, though in fact while thousands of Cumbrians did take to bicycles, something more devastating was brewing. Once the First World War had ended, bus companies sprang into being, operated by enterprising demobbed men who had learned to drive lorries when in the army and now were keen to put their skills to the test. The buses, as well as the growing number of cars, not only robbed the stagecoaches of their trade, but frequently created dangerous situations as the noisy vehicles overtook the horses on poor roads.

For many it proved too much. In 1921 Riggs sold up (see advert), and though others kept going, in particular Browns of Ambleside — who ran horse charabancs until the Second World War — the world of transport had changed forever.

The steamer has tied up at Glenridding pier after a trip round Ullswater and the horses wait as passengers prepare to continue their journey by stagecoaches. It is a hot day, as the brollies show. Less obvious is the alcoholic condition of the coach drivers who were noted for the enthusiasm with which they visited the bar at the nearby hotel while the steamer trips took place.

But at last they prepare to head south, back over Kirkstone Pass and on down to Ambleside and Windermere. The coaches usually passed Patterdale School about home-time and a battle of wits frequently took place as children sought to jump on to the back of the coaches and get free lifts for a mile or two up to Hartsop. Some drivers let them be, but others cracked their whips and brought the culprits tumbling.

Years after this scene, as motor cars began to multiply, the valley children played a game all of their own, sitting at the top of the pass and taking bets on how many cars would get over. Come 1912, the success rate of cars making it in one attempt was low. Car after car boiled, radiators were filled from the becks, and then long waits ensued while everything cooled down before trying again. The kids loved it.

A hundred feet (30m) above the rocky bed of the South Tyne river, a double-header passenger train, pulled by a J21 and a G5, crosses the spectacular Lambley Viaduct bound for Alston. In fact the passengers could hardly see the structure, which was only fourteen feet (4.25m) wide and barely visible from the carriages, giving a splendid feeling almost of floating on air.

Whitehaven, Cleator and Egremont Railway

ALTERATION OF TRAINS

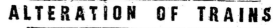

TIME and FARE TABLE, on and after the 1st Day of JULY. 1858.

Passenger Trains will be run as under :—
DOWN TRAINS.

STATIONS.	Week Days.			Sundays.		Fares fr Egremont		
	1st & 3d Class.	1st & 3d Class.	1st & 3d Class.	1st & 3d Class.	1st & 3d Class.	Ordinary. 1	3	Day. 1
Leave	A. M.	P. M.	P. M.	A. M.	P. M.	s. d.	s. d.	s. d.
Egremont	8 35	1 45	6 0	9 55	5 35	....	......	......
Woodend	8 40	1 50	6 5	10 0	5 40	0 3	0 1½	0 5
Frizington	8 25	1 35	5 50	9 30	5 10	0 9	0 4½	1 2
Cleator Moor.....................	8 30	1 40	5 55	9 35	5 15	0 7	0 3½	0 11
Moor Row Junction......	8 45	1 55	6 10	10 5	5 45	....	....	....
Ar. at Whaven (Corkickle Sta.)	9 0	2 15	6 25	10 20	6 5	1 0	0 6	1 6

Trains leave Whitehaven for Maryport, Carlisle, &c., at 10 5 A.M., 3 45 P.M., and 6 50 P.M.; and for Broughton, Ulverston. &c.. at 11 15 A.M.. and 5 10 P.M.

A Class 4 standard tank engine gusts smoke and steam on the Cockermouth, Keswick, Penrith Line, better known as the CKP. The line opened to passengers in 1865 and in late Victorian times, particularly, was exceedingly popular during the summer tourist seasons, inspiring the building of the Keswick Hotel. At Cockermouth, it was once possible to continue on by rail to Workington, but that route closed, and the final day for passengers between Penrith and Cockermouth came in March 1972. Rail enthusiasts still hope to reopen the CKP.

Usually it is the trains that move, but in this case it was the station. The old Wigton Station, opened in 1843, was a stop on the Maryport and Carlisle line but the day came when a new station was planned. The old one was dismantled and transported to Netherhall, Maryport, where it was re-erected as a summerhouse for the Senhouse family. As folk sometimes remark, they do things differently in Wigton.

A train steams across the Solway Firth Viaduct, in its day a journey regarded as a great adventure, and even more so once the viaduct began to fall to pieces. Built by the Solway Junction Railway, it bridged the firth for 1,940 yards (1,770m), without the embankments, and stretched from Annan on the Scottish side to the Cumberland village of Bowness. It opened to passengers in 1870, cost more than £100,000 and was regarded as a marvel of engineering. Large numbers of visitors journeyed to see the Lake District via this spectacular route.

But winters were the great enemy. Ice floes damaged the structure, the ice cracking and penetrating some of the hollow pillars. During the terrible winter of 1880, ice blocks sometimes up to ten feet (3m) thick filled the estuary, and by January 1881 two breaches had developed, one almost 300 yards (270m) wide. The viaduct was repaired and was back in use again from 1884 up to the First World War. From 1914 to 1920, light pig-iron trains crossed it, though no passengers. Gradually the viaduct fell into disrepair until only pedestrians used it, particularly Annan men who wanted a drink on Sundays when English pubs were open. Officially, though, it was closed at the end of 1921 as being dangerous and decidedly unsafe.

Not that everyone paid attention to that. Daredevil young Scots still saw the decaying structure as a challenge and a way to get a pint. They evaded the watchman and braved the Solway waters by jumping the gaping holes in the dark, a long dangerous trek to Bowness. A few were caught and fined but others were successful. The great adventure finally ended in 1934-5 when the viaduct was demolished

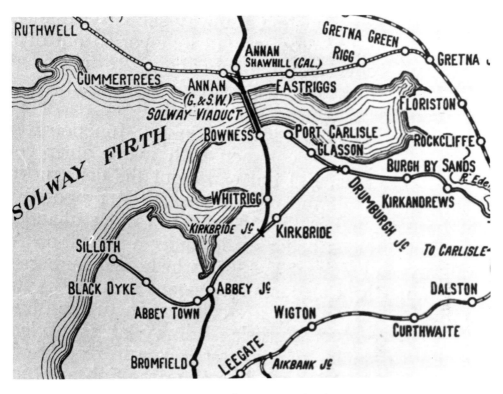

The route to adventure ... and a pint.

The gaping viaduct, damaged by ice floes.

Shiny and bright, the little steam engine *Devon* halts at Eskdale Station to pick up passengers. This bustling little rural railway delighted folk more than a century ago, and it still does. Its head lies inland in wild granite country, and its foot at the salt marshes of the coast. Really it's called the Ravenglass and Eskdale Railway, but that's too much for locals, who stick to La'al Ratty. Built with a three-feet (1m) gauge in 1875 to take iron ore to the coast from the mines at Boot, it soon carried passengers. The ore trade dwindled and later the line began to transport Eskdale granite. It was converted to a fifteen-inch (38cm) gauge in 1915, and runs seven miles (11km) from the main-line station on the coast at Ravenglass up to Eskdale Green. The Ratty has faced numerous frights, including dismal closure for a time, but it has survived all of them and steams on, a great day out.

A smart little railway engine — for only £760. This is from a catalogue of 1860, though the original Lowca works on the Cumbrian coast is believed to have been founded in 1763 to make brass cannons for merchant vessels. Several firms successively took over the works,. Locomotives were built for the Maryport and Carlisle Rilway, and later light locomotives for collieries, iron mines and ironworks,

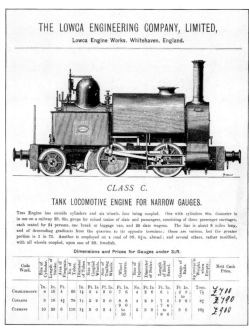

THE LOWCA ENGINEERING COMPANY, LIMITED,
Lowca Engine Works. Whitehaven, England.

CLASS C.

TANK LOCOMOTIVE ENGINE FOR NARROW GAUGES.

This Engine has outside cylinders and six wheels, four being coupled. One with cylinders 8in. diameter is in use on a railway 2ft. 8in. gauge for mixed trains of slate and passengers, consisting of three passenger carriages, each seated for 24 persons, one break or luggage van, and 20 slate wagons. The line is about 8 miles long, and of descending gradients from the quarries to its opposite terminus; these are various, but the greater portion is 1 in 75. Another is employed on a road of 3ft. 0¼in. abroad; and several others, rather modified, with all wheels coupled, upon one of 3ft. Swedish.

Dimensions and Prices for Gauges under 3ft.

Code Word	Size of Cylinder	Length of Stroke	No. of Tubes	Area of Firegrate	Diameter of Tubes	Size of Coupled Wheels	Size of Trailing Wheels	Wheel Centres	Size of Injector	Diameter of Boiler	Length of Boiler Barrel	Gauge of Rails	Approximate Weight when Empty	Nett Cash Price
	In.	In.	Ft.		In.	Ft. In.	Ft. In.	Ft. In.	No.	Ft. In.	Ft. In.	Ft. In.	Tons.	
CHARLEMAGNE	8	16	4	66	1¼	2 4	2 0	7 6	4	2 6	6 1	{ 2 3 to 3 6 }	7¾	£710
COOLENS	9	16	4½	78	1¼	2 9	2 0	{ 8 8, 9 0 }	4	2 9	{ 7 8, 7 6 }	3 6	8½	£790
CLEMENT	10	20	6	110	1½	3 0	2 4	{ 8 8, 9 0, to, 10 }	5	3 0	{ 7 6, 8 6 }	3 6	10½	£910

One railway engine at least failed to steam through Lindal in Furness. An 0-6-0 crossed onto this section and the track collapsed under it. Down went the engine along with bits of rail, an experience the engine's crew were lucky enough to relate for they managed to jump clear, and no doubt for long afterwards told the tale. It happened in 1892 and mining subsidence was blamed.

Two blasts of steam, and a double-header Scottish Express is all set to leave Carlisle Citadel Station. The station cost £178,000 and was designed by Sir William Tite in the sixteenth-century collegiate style.

The engine that fell into the South Tyne river. It happened in 1920 during the Newcastle and Carlisle Railway days and gave a young engineer cleaner the fright of his life.

Tank engine 60 DTP had been stabled at Alston locomotive shed after a night run, but unknown to cleaner Joe Palmley, who prepared to refill its bunker with coal ready for the morning journey, the fireman had over-filled the engine's boiler with water. The moment Joe took off the brakes and opened the regulator to head for the refilling point, he found himself in charge of a runaway engine. To his dismay, the regulator would not close against the pressure of the water. The runaway rumbled through the points and hit the safety run-off line. Joe jumped as the engine went over into the river, losing its chimney in the process. White about the gills, the cleaner knocked up the stationmaster to say that there would be no 7am engine that day. The engineers jacked up the engine, which was soon back in service and ran without further trouble. Joe was cleared of all blame, and went on to become an experienced and trusty driver.

Trains still operate at Alston, where the South Tynedale Railway Preservation Society runs a popular narrow-gauge line.

Cecil Oldfield was fourteen, and this was the first day in his first job as a learner clerk with the Furness Railway Company, 1912. Cecil shows off his uniform at Silecroft Station near Millom, and in particular the symbol of his new status, a railway watch and chain, part of the tradition of aiming to keep the trains running on time. The navy-blue melton uniform was supplied free by the company, and in the years ahead, each time Cecil needed a new outfit he was measured by Redmaynes, the tailoring firm at Wigton. Stiff collars were worn, usually celluloid, or linen, which was ironed until it went hard.

A job on the railways was regarded by many boys and their parents as highly desirable. There was an entrance exam before one became a junior clerk, and no pay for the first year. After that it was 7s 6d (37½p) a week, rising to 10s 6d (52½p) in the third year. Cecil gave his wages to his mother, keeping 6d (2½p) a week for pocket money.

Several others members of the Oldfield family were in rail service, including Cecil's father, Harry, who was the stationmaster at Silecroft when his son began to work there. Cecil rose to become stationmaster at Eskmeals, Threlkeld and elsewhere. Later, as a relief stationmaster, he ranged from Carlisle to Blackpool. In 1959 he retired and received a gold railway watch for loyally keeping the trains running and, wherever humanly possible, to time.

The motor age has dawned and the new motorised generation halts in the road at Alston. If mechanically everything looks intriguingly antique, the motors would seem modern enough the day this picture was taken. Even the Golden Lion has been quick to latch on, with a promise of accommodation for cyclists and motorists. Plus a large motor shed. Such sheds were usually former stables, which in the larger hotels were advertised as capable of holding up to 100 horses.

Opposite:

Carlisle tanker driver Joseph Rowley, right, of Wapping, Carlisle, and two workmates test the fuel level in this impressive solid-looking carrier, seen at its Currock depot. Bulk deliveries of motor spirit (Petrol was a brand name in the early days) were made in and around the city, and whatever else might happen, there was never any problem about punctures. The first pneumatic-tyred tanker operated by BP was an AEC, bought in 1924, but there was a degree of scepticism about pneumatic tyres on heavier lorries and this persisted through the 1920s, so Joseph was doing all right with solid tyres. The wheels on the tanker are a type seen on some Karrier lorries, and that may well be its make.

A familiar delivery van in and around Ulverston back in 1915 was this Ford Tin Lizzie. At the wheel in a straw hat is Mr R Quine, whose bakery and confectionary shop was at 29 Market Street. He was born at that address and was a baker for fifty-seven years.

The van, with its solid tyres, had oil-burning sidelights, while the headlights burned acetylene gas fed from the container on the running board. The vehicle was a hand-cranked job with no screenwashers, and was reported to have been the first commercial van in the town.

Mr Quine's father started Quine's bakery, taking over the premises from a biscuit maker, J B Martin. The young Mr Quine stepped in when he was twenty. He and his staff started each night at eleven and worked until eleven the next morning, turning out about a ton of bread each time, some 2,240 lb (1,015kg). Back in 1906 a large Quine loaf cost 2d (1p), but by 1914 the cost of living was rising and it had gone up to 4½d (2p). Wherever would it end?

Coach owner Edgar Hadwin of Ulverston about to set off on an excursion in the 1920s. However efficient the vehicle's hood, folded away at the back, experienced travellers knew that it was usually wise to insure against the Lakeland cold, hence the generous layers of heavy coats.

Bus services sprouted across Britain after the First World War, and among the resourceful Cumbrian bus operators was Edgar Hadwin, who started his firm in 1919, buying old chassis and building his own coachwork. His firm thrived and eventually he was able to buy new buses, so that by the 1970s he had a superb fleet of ten luxury coaches which he sold to John Shaw and Son (Silverdale). One journey he remembered in particular …

The worst bus trip I ever had, well that was the first time I drove up from Poole in Dorset with a Siddeley Deasy. Cost me anything up to £60. I was a bit of a mechanic, really, bought me buses mainly in bits.

There was a paper printed in them days and I saw this one advertised, so I went to look at it and see what it was worth. When I got to Poole, it was standing in a garage without tyres. There was no garages to speak of then. I bought tubes at one place; it was the only blooming thing the feller had for sale. Then I set off for the North; sat at the steering in the open in the rain, wrapped up, no mudguards or anything like that, hardly any lights. Travelled mainly by day, no more than twenty miles [35km] an hour. Couldn't travel at night because I'd nowt working except me engine. And I came up the Great North Road, and in places there was still grass growing up in the middle of it; sitting out in the open, be about 1923. I bought meself a big pie to eat and had nothing but me big coat to keep me warm and it took me four days to fetch it up to Ulverston.

There was little traffic, except horse-drawn ones. Must be 350 miles [560km] from Poole. Roads were terrible. Signposts had been pulled down in places, because of the

Great War. I lost me way a few times. You had to stop to read what it said on the signposts. They were that small lettering. You couldn't read 'em when moving; not big enough letters. I'd only got me bike lamp, acetylene, and a box for a seat.

Oh, I'd a hell of a lot of punctures on the run, and for some reason, can't remember what, instead of going to Ulverston I went on to Kendal and got lost. It was getting late, see. I couldn't find me way out of Kendal. The engine needed water badly, so I got into a yard and come across a scrap heap and there was a bucket in it. I looked at this bucket and thought it was all right. I was there when a policeman found me and eyed me up. I put the bucket in the cab and said: 'That'll do to fill her up!' Well he laughed and took me up to the police station and filled it with water from a pipe there.

When I got home to Ulverston a feller as worked for me said: 'What've you fetched this for?' It was the bucket.

I said: 'I don't know. I wanted to fill up with water.'

He says: 'Nay, there's no bottom in it!'

I just hadn't looked at it proper. That bucket was kicking around for years.

Tysons coal lorry and a friendly dog at Caldbeck in the 1920s. The vehicle had many uses: carrying stone for the new village bridge, flittings, moving sheep and, when suitably converted, carrying passengers. There was no glass in the windows, but there were blinds to keep out the weather.

Its most memorable load was a hefty bull. Wooden sides were fitted to the lorry and the beast was hauled into place, at which point it was found that the engine was not strong enough to climb up the hill out of the village. Everything started over again. The bull was unloaded and walked up to the top where it was reloaded, and off they went. Out of these pioneering beginnings, Tysons thrived and today is a successful coach firm.

Everything seems calm enough, a paddle steamer coming alongside in Bowness Bay, Windermere. A few years earlier, however, Windermere had been the scene of a fierce steamer war waged by two rival boat companies.

The Windermere Steam Yacht Company was the first on the scene, launching the *Lady of the Lake* in 1845. In the company's first season 5,000 passengers were carried, and this success did not go unnoticed. A rival company, the Windermere Iron Steam Boat Company, launched two iron paddlers, *Firefly* in 1849, and *Dragonfly* in 1850, and a battle to attract passengers began. Price-cutting started, clashes broke out ashore among rival crew members, and vessels struggled to get into the best pick-up points. Then in 1850, the original company's steamer, the *Lord of the Isles*, went up in flames in Bowness Bay. Arson was suspected, though it was never proven. Other incidents followed, until eventually the two companies decided that the sensible solution to the conflict was to amalgamate. In 1866 the new company, the Windermere United Yacht Co, launched the *Rothay*, seen here in calm waters, and in 1869 the first *Swan*. With everything calmer, tourism picked up. The new set-up was a success, and once again this did not go unnoticed.

In 1872 the burgeoning Furness Railway officially took over the steamers, with a rail link to Lakeside at the foot of Windermere. Four more vessels were launched: the *Teal*, 1879; the *Cygnet*, 1879; the *Tern*, 1891; and the *Swift*, 1900. Day trips to Lakeland with a sightseeing steamer outing included were exceedingly popular with visitors.

But one thing often seems to swallow up another, and in 1923 the Furness Railway was incorporated into the London, Midland and Scottish Railway, which launched two more vessels, the *Teal II* in 1936, and *Swan II* in 1938.

Numerous other changes followed, including nationalisation and privatisation, so that today the whole operation is run by Windermere Lake Cruises. Three of the vessels still ply up and down the ten and a half mile (17km) lake, the *Tern*, the *Swan II* and the *Teal II*. All are now diesel driven, though passengers can arrive adventurously at Lakeside Station by steam train on the Lakeside and Haverthwaite Railway.

A busy boating scene at Lakeside Station, at the foot of Windermere. The steamer *Swift* has just left its mooring alongside the tea pavilion and is setting off north up the lake. The station, part of Furness Railway, made a splendid landmark and became a familiar sight to thousands of visitors. This postcard was sent on the 30th August 1905 to a Miss M Blizard of Roman Road, Bemerton, Salisbury, and the writer, who signed himself Budge, told her 'Went to Windermere today' and 'Got a pot for you of Ambleside'. On the front, he added 'Boat I went by' and 'Were [sic] I had lunch while the band played'.

Troops come off the Windermere Ferry and check the load. Before steam arrived, the old ferries were propelled by long wooden sweeps, or oars, and the craft seemed small in comparison with the new metal jobs. In Bowness the locals greeted the first steam ferry as 'a great gert battleship'. And subsequent larger replacements earned a similar description. The ferry service is some 600 years old.

At one time just about every-body in and around Bowness and Windermere knew this spry fellow, Johnny Atkinson, the Windermere ferryman. He was renowned for his dry wit, and if some of the tales about him have grown with the telling they are usually worth hearing. Typical was the day a late passenger ran down the old Lancashire side slipway calling urgently for the ferry to come back. It was several feet out but the man, eyeing the gap, risked all and jumped, landing in a heap on the deck.

'Eeh! I thought as I'd not make it', he gasped.

'Aye', said Johnny agreeably. He helped the man to his feet. 'Just coming in.'

Johnny worked for the ferry service for some twenty-seven years, and in 1910 or so was paid 21s (£1.05) for a seven-day week, 'plus a free meal'.

The ferry had an intimate atmosphere, especially at day-end when a blast on the steam whistle signalled the last crossing. Paraffin lamps lit the cabins and storm lanterns the deck. A combined smell of coal, smoke and paraffin encompassed a motley range of passengers who included labourers on most days, and at other times gypsies, cows, bulls, donkeys, sheep, stagecoaches, organ grinders with monkeys, beer drays, loads of wood and occasional funerals. One of the oddest passengers arrived the day a man and his dancing bear wanted to cross. A row broke out because bears did not appear to be on the ferry's long list of charges. In the end Johnny put it down as a donkey.

In its time the ferry has gone adrift (ending down-lake towards Storrs Hall), has become stuck on its cable-haul, rammed the occasional tree trunk, and even unexpectedly gone into reverse.

The older ferries had no shelter. As Johnny said: 'Them days? Nay, it would a been drier in t' lake!'

Many fine private vessels have sailed on Windermere, and here is Mr Higgins and his family with their steam craft the *Undine,* which was to be seen about the 1880s–1890s plying up and down the lake.

Sometimes these vessels arrived in the Lakes from long distances, an example being another fine craft, the *Britannia,* which was owned by Colonel G J M Ridehalgh of Fell Foot, Windermere. His vessel was built by T B Seath of Rutherglen and arrived in sections by rail at Windermere. There is an old story that some parts of the *Britannia* were simply too big to get under one of the bridges between Rutherglen and Lakeland, and so they were transported on a Sunday, that being the quietest day. Twin sections of the rail line under the bridge were rapidly dug up and re-laid as a single track until the big bits were through, then the twin track was re-laid ready for Monday's trains. Perhaps the bridge had a curved arch, reducing the squared width. Once at Windermere Station the sections were carted down to the lake, and the craft was assembled and launched. Well, it's a good story.

Opposite:
Lines of men launch Seascale lifeboat through the shallows into the Irish Sea. It was a hard haul before deep water was reached, and the wheels had to be fitted with flat boards to prevent the launching trolley from sinking. The crew used to live at Whitehaven, miles distant. When a ship was in distress, the SOS was relayed by telegraph to Whitehaven, and the coastguards and the lifeboat crew ran to catch the train at Bransty station. Once they had reached Seascale, they still had to race down to the sea.

'White one way, black the other' — that used to be the saying when people spoke about the Kendal to Lancaster Canal. The barge plying the quiet waters at Hest Bank scarcely indicates the important trade link the canal once provided for the Westmorland town.

The canal was built in 1815-18 at a reputed cost of more than £600,000. The intention had been to link Kendal with the Wigan coalfield, though it reached no farther than Preston. Even so, it was a great asset. Barges took out considerable quantities of limestone and much else, while the reverse trade saw almost all the coal for Kendal and South Westmorland brought in. Hence the saying. Usually two horses pulled each coal barge and were changed every four miles (6.5km).

At the opening in 1819 a grand procession of sixteen packets and boats went to Kendal. At one stage there was even an express passenger return service from Preston, the fifty-seven-or-so mile (90km) journey taking about seven hours. Capacity was seventy people and the fares were 4s (20p) to 6s (30p).

At Whitsuntide, parties of Sunday school children filled the boats. They sang as they sailed to Hincaster, where they got out and walked to Levens Park for a picnic.

Masts and spars crowd Silloth Docks on the Solway coast. The dock opened in 1859 with high hopes among its Victorian designers, who saw the planned town as a port and a pleasant seaside resort. Passenger services existed to Dublin, the Isle of Man and Liverpool, though the port found it difficult to compete with the facilities at Workington and Whitehaven. The last fully-rigged sailing ships at Silloth are said to have been there about the time of the First World War. In 1913 they included a German vessel with wheat from Australia for Carrs Mills. The harbour is still in use, importing and exporting goods.

A paddle tugboat lies alongside the quay in Workington Harbour. The harbour has played an important part in the West Cumbrian town's history and owes its development to the iron, steel and coal industries

The February storms raged and several ships off the Cumbrian coast were reported to be in difficulty. One of them was the lightship *Selker* which was washed ashore on Drigg beach. It happened one morning in 1903 and though there was damage, the vessel was still upright and a ladder was needed to climb down to the shingle when supplies were delivered.

Rural Moments

MANY OF THE pictures in this book qualify as part of rural life, but here are a few of the especially appealing and somewhat poignant ones. A brilliant picture out of the past is that of the Drigg parish councillors, opposite. Such steadfast expressions, such strong jaws. How reassuring it must have been with such determined-looking guardians of the parish around.

And the story of Anne Moffat — that too seems to capture much of the old Cumbrian way of life. On a winter's day we drank tea in her little parlour at Lorton where she recalled her cycling adventures delivering letters, and how she had concealed the mince pies at Christmas. And her struggle with a drunken postman … the last alone makes her story worth knowing.

Yet of all the pictures, perhaps the most evocative is the funeral procession of the Flookburgh fishermen. The photo is dark, and rather hard to make out, but the tragedy of the loss of three of the village's young men and what it meant to that little community can readily be sensed as the solemn lines of mourners walk with the coffins to the graveyard, their eyes downcast.

Drigg Parish Council outside Drigg Vicarage, 1894-5. Stability and assuredness exude from the faces of these parish worthies, dressed as they are in their best Victorian clothes with boots well polished and hard hats doffed.

Parish councils were a new thing and in places replaced church vestries. The parish records in this case show their names, though not the order, with five of them called John. They are John Bailiff, Abraham Brocklebank, John Cook, William Hodgkin, John Pearson, Ruben B Roberts, John Thompson (Sandyford), and John Wrigley.

For half a century and possibly longer this picture, along with many more related ones, has scarcely seen daylight. For years it lay forgotten under a Lakeland staircase, and could easily have been lost forever but for the keen eyes of a vicar's widow who recognised their worth and saved them. It is from a collection of 120 or so lantern slides taken by Kenneth Pughe, son of the Rev K M Pughe who was the vicar at Drigg at the turn of the last century. Back in 1894-5, Kenneth seems to have set out with his camera, almost as if on a mission to record a moment of time, for he began to photograph the local people in an area covered mainly by Irton, Santon, Holmrook, Drigg and Carleton in what is now west Cumbria. Most of the people he photographed were taken standing outside their own homes, either in their best or their working clothes. The gentry, too, are well represented. It is a parish captured on glass, with skating scenes, cycling, sledding, golf and tennis players, school groups, bell ringers, stonebreakers, maids and blacksmiths, even an old woman with her parrot in a cage at her cottage door.

The slides came to light again when they were found in their boxes amid a pile of hymn books under the stairs at Drigg Vicarage and were rescued by Mrs Ruth Moore, widow of the Rev George Moore, who had been the vicar of that parish. Today Kenneth Pughe's photo mission of long ago is stored safely in the Cumbrian county's records office, worthy of a book in its own right.

A horse, its mane beautifully plaited, stands spruce and shiny as the judges are awaited at Hesket Newmarket show.

Some tails are up, but others are definitely playing it cool, as well they might when you find yourself being walked out in the middle of Windermere on a freezing winter's day with scarcely a decent scent in range.

An extraordinary winter, still called the Great Freeze, seized Lakeland in 1894-5. Windermere turned into a vast sheet of ice, some nine inches (23cm) thick, not a totally unblemished surface for the whole of its ten or so miles (16km) — one man went through and was drowned — but a tremendous place for skating. Thousands did, even by moonlight, arriving in special excursion trains at Windermere station in their legions. Bonfires were built on the ice, and sleds were pushed out loaded with glowing chestnut braziers. A coach and four horses drove regularly over Bowness Bay to Belle Isle and people paid 2d (1p) a ride to say they had been across the lake on ice.

The freeze lasted for almost seven weeks with minor thaws. When the ice began to break, the cracking sounded like cannons being fired.

The Moffat family outside their post office at High Lorton.

She was called Anne Moffat and she was young, soft spoken and gentle mannered, and for years she cycled and walked in the beautiful Vale of Lorton, near Cockermouth, delivering letters and parcels on her beloved Swift bicycle. She braved winter storms, snowdrifts and long treks to lonely farms in the wilds around Buttermere and Crummock Water. She loved her job and was much liked by the fell community she served. It all happened before the First World War when her parents kept High Lorton post office and her mother baked teacakes three times a week to help pay their way. She found an especially favourite photograph …

You are looking here at High Lorton post office. That's my father on the right, John Moffat. The boy's called Robert, the old lady's my grandmother … now then, I'll have forgot what we called her … Oh, I shouldn't have forgotten my grandmother's name, should I? It'll likely come back. The tall lady is my mother, Elizabeth, then there's me, Anne, and Hannah, my sister on the left.

I wasn't even born when mother and father took on the shop. Father was a shoemaker down at Low Lorton first. Then Lorton Hall was rebuilt and the little cottage he worked in was pulled down and he came up to High Lorton, opposite this post office.

There was a shop at this spot before mother and father took it on, but nobody could make it pay, and people belonging the next house, the Musgraves, had an aunty in and they built her a brick oven to make bread to help out. Well that didn't do it, so it stood empty a long time till Mr Musgrave said to my father wouldn't he start the shop, and no he didn't think he could but he would mention it to mother, and mother said: 'Oh no, I'm not going in, anybody who's been in, they've come out worse than they went in.' But Mr Musgrave went on bothering father and they thought they would try, so mother went to Cockermouth and she'd £5 to spend to start a shop and she got little bits of things, you know, and she started it.

The room just inside was the shop. You just came in at a door and along one wall we had bins for flour in sacks. Across on the other was where we cut bacon and cheese and had tins of biscuits. There was little cupboards where mother stored jams and pickles; and shelves with sweets; and a bit higher up, packets of starch, packets of cornflour, anything in packets. In the corner was tin tacks.

On one side were little old-fashioned drawers with brass knobs which I used to clean. The bottom one was deeper with elastic and safety pins, and the next perhaps had saltpetre because people used to cure their own bacon; and another had candles. The middle drawers, well I can't remember everything, but I remember the top had white pepper in one drawer and black pepper in another because they made us sneeze.

Mother and father brought up our family on this shop and the shoemaker's. But we had to work because the post office paid only £2 18s 6d [£2.93] a month for keeping it. There was just a few stamps, a few postal orders. Then they got the savings bank.

We used to bake teacakes three times a week and they sold well. Bigger families then. Nearly everybody had four or six children. I started working in the shop soon as

I left Lorton School at fourteen. The shop was open long hours and if you were closed people came to the kitchen door. We'd to open about 7.30am because the postman called with a horse and trap and came to see if there was letters to go.

We had a telephone instrument, not the old-fashioned ABC instrument, ours was a telephone because it was much easier. Ten o'clock every morning you had to answer it to see if your clock was right with everybody else. 'Are you there Lorton? Are you there Loweswater?' You said: 'Yes.' In a second or two it was ten o'clock. You'd to time telegrams when you received them. And then you had to deliver 'em. You were allowed about five minutes, and who went with it. And if it was over a mile you'd to put whether you'd walked or whether you'd cycled, and you got 6d [2½p] over a mile; and 9d [3¾p] over a mile and a half. In any kind of weather from eight in the morning till eight at night. We didn't think it was hard because we were brought up to it.

In their best outfits, three of the Moffat children, Hannah, Anne and Robert.

Both my sister and I had a round for taking letters. I should have been sixteen but seeing we'd had the post office so long, I was about fifteen, and they let me, which was a privilege. Two hours a day, Mondays to Saturdays. My round was 4s [20p] a week, two hours walking a morning. I set off for Lorton and all the outlying places up to High Swinside, down to Low Swinside on to Hope, then Miller Place, and back by High Mill and all round. Walking, and I wanted to be back soon … And I wanted a bicycle!

You had to find your own bicycle. They cost a lot of money. My first cost £10, bought it in Irvings in Cockermouth. I know I fought for years for a bicycle. Father had some outstanding bills and he said if I went to Lanthwaite Green and took this bill for some shoes he'd done and not got paid for I could put what I got towards a bicycle. He says I'd to say: 'Please, my father has sent you this bill and he's very sorry that unless you can let him have something off it by Monday he'll have to put you in county court.' So I got so much back off that bill. Oh, I came back very pleased. And I had to go to another place and got a bit paid off there too.

I said to my father: 'I can have me bike now.'

'What', he says, 'this won't buy you a bike!'

It wasn't much I'd got. But he helped me get one. A Swift, when I was sixteen. It just had a little oil lamp; but you weren't out often after dark. The roads were too bad. Felt safer walking. I had to sign a paper that if I had an accident cycling I would not claim off the Post Office.

My sister got 2s 6d [12½p] for her round. Hers was an hour and a quarter. She had to go up the Whinlatter road twice a week; then it got to be three times a week. Things just grew. Letters got more and more. My parents got savings bank and licences. Then first time, the old-age pension. The old lady who lived up the steps came in and got her money. And she says: 'Now how long do you think this'll last — getting money for nowt!'

I started delivering letters on my bike about 1899 or 1900. It was a long way. I wouldn't know how far it was. Sometimes you'd feel: Well, I won't push my bike down that spot, 'cause you'd to bring it back. And you'd maybe walk that bit.

Delivering in snow was bad. Had to wear your clogs mostly. I used to have to cut the roads with a shovel to get through. And sometimes couldn't get letters up to the houses by the fells. Too steep for a bicycle, and too slippy. But come summer and I even went on a ride to Silloth. Not post office business. Went to see the pierrots, you know. Two others went, too, those with a bike. We were terrible late back and father was worried.

We didn't wear a uniform doing letters, but eventually we had a brown badge to put on our arm with GPO. Didn't wear mine. Sometimes the inspector used to go round with you, just to see that we took the time we said we did. But he didn't go to all the houses. If you hadn't a letter for one he'd say: 'Oh, well, we'll not go down there. That'll be

More Agents Sell
More Riders Recommend

SWIFT

CYCLES

Than any other make of Cycles in the World, because they are the best.
—:o:—
ALSO OTHER MAKES OF GOOD REPUTE.

Maker of the "Egremont Castle" Cycle.

Tyres, Accessories, and Repairs of all kinds
Liberal Discounts to Cash Buyers,   Lists Post Free.

H. LEWTHWAITE,
CASTLE CYCLE WORKS,
EGREMONT.

Anne Moffat's first bicycle was a Swift, recommended in this advertisement from the 1890s.

ten minutes or so.' He had a watch to time you and a list of all the houses.

We had some awful do's. We used to have a postman over from Loweswater to call at the shop for our mail. We had a letterbox in the window. We used to fasten up a canvas bag and seal it with some wax and give it to this postman. Joe. He got drunk one day after Loweswater Show, oh, and he didn't come to collect the letters. You know he was gifted with getting drunk. He was rather bad tempered. We rung Loweswater and said: 'Has Joe come?' She says: 'Well, yes — oh, he is drunk. There's a man riding down with him.'

We were having the house painted and I says to the painter: 'Do you think Joe will be drunk?' And he says: 'Yes, he's sure to be.' And I says: 'Oh dear, I don't know what to do.'

So I rung Cockermouth and a woman says: 'What time should he be there?' And I says: 'Quarter past four.' She says: 'It's nearly quarter past five! What's happened?' I says: 'We think he's had an accident.'

Then Joe came after a bit. He got out of his trap and could hardly stand. I says: 'Oh, you are late. They're asking about you at Cockermouth.' And he says: 'What did you say?' 'I said you hadn't come.'

Then the phone rung and it was Mr Riley. I says: 'Mr Riley says are you all right? Wants to know if you are drunk.' And Joe says: 'Nooo, tell him I's not drunk!' So Mr Riley says: 'Is he drunk?' And I says: 'He says he isn't.'

Anyway I said I'd go along on me bike with him and Mr Riley said that was all right. So off we set. Oh, he was in a pickle. Joe knew the boxes but couldn't get the keys into them to open up, and I said: 'If you give me the keys I'll open up and give you all that's in. Will that do?'

'Oh, aye, that'll do', he says, and we worked like that all the way to Cockermouth. Anyway, Joe went to the post office in Cockermouth and was going to hit the postmaster. Oh, there was such a do! He was nearly retired, but the schoolmaster got a petition up, and in the end he got his job back and kept his pension.

It was good being a post-lady. Everyone was friendly. If it was a wet morning they give you a cup of tea. One old lady, when she was well, always had a teacake and a piece of cheese for me. I wasn't hungry but I had to take it. Christmas was worst when they said: 'Come in, and have your pie.' And you had to eat it. It wouldn't be so bad if you could put it in your bag and take it home, but sitting down and having this and ginger wine with it. You nearly had to be walking out through the doorpost.

You got sixpence for your Christmas box. And you knew where you'd get sixpence, and there were two places where you got a shilling. You got mince pies till you grew tired; but you'd to sit and eat them and talk, and you'd your letters to get on with! Aeeey. But they were never wasted. Mince pies! I hid 'em inside my blouse, even when they were hot, and brought them home; you had them warmed up again for your dinner instead of pudding, you know.

Christmas Day deliveries was awful; letters were late coming. And big parcels to deliver. You got 12lb [5.5kg] weight for a shilling [5p]. They were heavy. I'd a flat on the back of my bike and fastened them on with straps. Sometimes I'd to cycle eight miles [13km] with the Buttermere post and once I fell into the hedge.

I gave up delivering when the First World War was over. I was told I would only be needed another week. You know, the men came back from the fighting and had to have work and they altered the Post Office and gave the soldiers the jobs. Only fair, really. My round was handed over. And the parishioners gave me a clock: 'Presented to Miss Anne Moffat as an appreciation of her 23 years' postal service. August 1921.' Twenty-three years biking and walking!

A country vet, John Martin Watson, well dressed with a shiny hat and strong boots, takes it easy outside his surgery with a copy of the *Veterinary Journal*. He lived at Rothery House, Ireby, more than a hundred years ago.

Fully qualified vets were not exactly over-plentiful in rural Cumbria at that time, though there were numerous skilled farmers who practised a mix of well-tried animal cures, along with other less effective methods which occasionally came close to superstition. Even in my own time I have seen a magic sixpence used in an attempt to charm ringworm out of a child's nose.

John Watson, however, set out to be fully qualified. He and his sister Annie were orphans and brought up by John Armstrong, an unqualified vet at Bothel. John Watson was apprenticed to Armstrong and got a liking for the work. He went to Edinburgh University and helped to pay his way during the vacations by long sessions turnip picking. In 1873 he became a fully qualified member of the Royal College of Veterinary Surgeons, though alas, while most of his fellow surgeons celebrated in style, near-penniless John could afford nothing more to eat than a single herring. It was a tale his wife loved to tell.

Ireby was John's first and only practice. For more than thirty years he was a successful country vet, travelling the rounds by pony and cart. He had an unqualified assistant, Rayson Cape from Torpenhow, and apart from their skills in veterinary medicine, they acquired a reputation for emergency dentistry. John and Rayson would carry a big leather armchair out into the surgery yard, and while Rayson gripped the victim's head from behind, John pulled any troublesome teeth. The sideline made little profit, for the victims were usually given a double whisky as consolation.

The crowd isn't large, though in rural terms the event is important enough, a sale at the Black Lion Inn in the High Furness village of Oxen Park. There is an unhurried air: a dog lying in the dust, folk standing at a distance from the business of the day; men dressed up, chatting.

The Black Lion was a popular venue for sales, and noted for its hospitality. The landlord at this time was T S Ormandy, and part of his living came from the hire of post horses as well as the sale of ale, wines, spirits and tobacco. Innkeepers in remote areas might also combine their job as host with a bit of farm labouring, or as a roadman, or a drystone waller. When times were bad, you worked where you could.

In 1900 eight people lived at the Black Lion. It was sold in 1910 and today has become two homes. Elsewhere in the village, two of the blacksmiths that once had horses queueing as late as ten at night waiting to be shod have gone; so too have the old carts. But there is still an inn, the Manor House, across the road where the garden wall shows.

Numerous tales about the local blacksmiths exist. A car full of people screeched to a halt one summer's evening and the driver stuck out his head and yelled: 'Hey mister, is this the Grizedale road?' Not quite the way you do it in Cumbria.

The blacksmith turned slowly, his face impassive. 'Aye', he said.

The driver engaged the gears, but to make sure, he shouted again: 'How long will it take us to get there?'

'Oh', said the blacksmith. 'Tha'll never *get* theer.' And he waved an arm to show what he meant. 'Tha's pointing wrong road.'

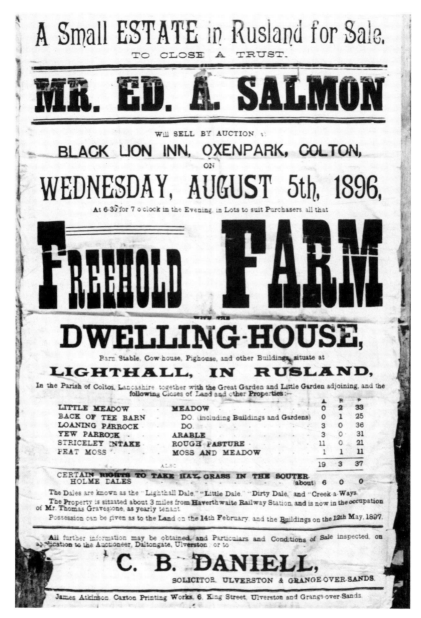

A Small ESTATE in Rusland for Sale.
TO CLOSE A TRUST.

MR. ED. A. SALMON

Will SELL BY AUCTION :

BLACK LION INN, OXENPARK, COLTON,

ON

WEDNESDAY, AUGUST 5th, 1896,

At 6-30 for 7 o'clock in the Evening, in Lots to suit Purchasers all that

FREEHOLD FARM

WITH THE

DWELLING-HOUSE,

Barn Stable, Cow-house, Pighouse, and other Buildings, situate at

LIGHTHALL, IN RUSLAND,

In the Parish of Colton, Lancashire together with the Great Garden and Little Garden adjoining, and the following Closes of Land and other Properties :—

			A	R	P
LITTLE MEADOW	MEADOW		0	2	33
BACK OF THE BARN	DO. (including Buildings and Gardens)		0	1	25
LOANING PARROCK	DO.		3	0	36
YEW PARROCK	ARABLE		3	0	31
STRICELEY INTAKE	ROUGH PASTURE		11	0	21
PEAT MOSS	MOSS AND MEADOW		1	1	11
	ALSO		19	3	37

CERTAIN RIGHTS TO TAKE HAY, GRASS IN THE SOUTER
HOLME DALES (about) 6 0 0

The Dales are known as the "Lighthall Dale," "Little Dale," "Dirty Dale," and "Creek-a-Ways."
The Property is situated about 3 miles from Haverthwaite Railway Station, and is now in the occupation of Mr. Thomas Gravestone, as yearly tenant.
Possession can be given as to the Land on the 14th February, and the Buildings on the 12th May, 1897.

All further information may be obtained, and Particulars and Conditions of Sale inspected, on application to the Auctioneer, Daltongate, Ulverston, or to

C. B. DANIELL,

SOLICITOR. ULVERSTON & GRANGE-OVER-SANDS.

James Atkinson, Carton Printing Works, 6, King Street, Ulverston and Grange-over-Sands.

It was always a social event when a farm was auctioned. The one in this poster, Lighthall in Rusland Valley, was to be sold at the Black Lion Inn, Oxen Park, in August 1896. It comprised of the house and outbuildings, along with a stable, a cow house, a pig house and other buildings. In all, a decent-sounding farm.

The poster points up the naming of fields around farms, which often pre-date mapping. Little Meadow and Back of the Barn, as shown here, like other field names frequently came about through practical usage and the need to identify the day's grazing, and other spots. A few chosen at random elsewhere in the Lake District include Old Cow Ditch, the Long Cut, Bessy's Bank, Old John's Intake and, a favourite, Wild Ducks Meadow. Thousands of similar names surely await the researchers.

A fishing community in mourning. A grey November in 1912 as the bodies of two fishermen are carried through the village of Flookburgh on the shores of Morecambe Bay. Mourners in caps and bowlers walk the rough stone road to the burial ground where the men were interred, victims of the sea. But this was only part of the story, for a third man was still missing.

A few days earlier the three young men, brothers Thomas and Edward Robinson, and a cousin, Frank Robinson, were caught in a gale out in the vastness of the bay while musselling. As other boats fled to shelter, the Robinson boat ran aground and broke up.

News of the disaster reached the village and the fathers of the three fishermen, accompanied by the vicar, caught a train to Ulverston and began a grim search along the shore. They found the bodies of Edward and Frank lying near Baycliffe, a few miles from home, but of Thomas there was no sign. On the 11th the cousins were buried and no one had much hope of finding the third fisherman.

What happened days later has become folklore. The bay, twelve miles (19km) across at its widest, is fed by the rivers Leven and Kent and

The grab which scooped up the body.

churned by the Irish Sea. On the 18th November the dredger *Hessam*, working with three grabs, was clearing the channel outside Heysham harbour, nine miles (14km) from Roosebeck Scar where the Robinsons had gone aground. The *Hessam* scooped up sand and mud for about an hour when one of the crew saw something strange about one of the grabs and signalled to the master to stop. To their consternation they found they had scooped up the body of a man, and it proved to be that of Thomas Robinson. It lay enclosed within the grab, as one eyewitness reported, untouched by the teeth 'as if in a cradle'. The bay extends to 122,000 acres (49,400ha) or more, the grab covers just four square yards (3.3m²).

Thomas, who was twenty-seven, left a wife and an infant daughter. He was buried at Flookburgh eleven days after drowning.

A moment of rural bliss. The heavily clothed passengers have stopped for refreshments outside the Masons Arms at Strawberry Bank, Cartmel Fell. The coach is from the Commercial Livery Stables in Kendal and charabanc outings with a suitable halt at the Masons were popular runs, despite the rough roads which often provided the passengers with plenty of bumps and jolts, as well as generous wafts of dust. Hats, veils and plenty of padding were seen by the lady passengers as being important.

The landlord was a John James Matthews and his sign declares that he is fully licensed to sell ale, beer, porter and foreign and British spirits.

Running a rural inn was not always highly profitable, but the more enterprising landlords tried to ensure that parties on coach outings were especially well treated, sometimes providing a staging post for a change of horses.

On the Road

THE OPEN ROADS SO often seemed to be empty, yet somewhere there, a little beyond the horizon, was a constant cavalcade of people always on the move. And from time to time they came into sight. Pedlars with trunks of fairings; drovers bound for distant markets, driving geese or cattle; or barrel-organ grinders, their performing monkeys, in a red jacket and skirt, collecting the pennies. There were gypsies, too, with their lucky heather, ready to swap pots and pans for rabbit skins.

Crowds were rare. More usually a lone figure would be at the door. Some days a knife grinder with a rough old cart, seemingly a one-wheeled affair, but which, turned over, revealed a second wheel sandstone-bright for sharpening knives. Or an old woman would knock, her pram loaded with red rudd stone for sale at farms and cottages, dug out of the riverbeds, for brightening doorsteps and windowsills.

Weekdays, it was the postman, walking miles, or pushing his bike along the rough bits. When the First World War robbed the community of its young men, postwomen took over, keeping things going, sometimes with inspectors to check that letters were properly timed. Checking, too, that the higher-spirited postmen, the Oldies who were still left, were not imbibing along the route.

Frequently tramps trudged through, begging. Men down out of Scotland, wanting work; or others across from the North-East, sometimes several together, in groups, walking along, occasionally scaring remoter communities as they approached. Wariness and tramps so often seemed to go together. At times, though, the reverse. Near Mungrisdale, exceptionally, a welcoming barn lay open to them, a tramps' barn where they could get a good kip for the night and be given a bowl of hot soup. In its time the barn was known up and down the land, and the generosity of its owners is remembered to this day, locally at least.

Most weeks, farmers' wives were off to market by pony and trap, though there were plenty who walked; or else their husbands were there droving sheep or cattle, their cur dogs circling endlessly.

In among this cavalcade came the circuses, horse-drawn wagons, sometimes in small convoys, to set up at Windermere, or Keswick or beyond.

Each in its turn, each to its season. And sometimes, even in the remotest hamlets, a true marvel, rising on its two hind legs, a bear dancing in the dust, on a chain, nowadays a poignant image, but in its own time part of the cavalcade.

A whiskery stare from Jimmy Dyer, fiddle player and ballad singer. For years Jimmy trailed the Cumbrian roads playing and singing, until at one time no fair seemed to be complete unless his weather-beaten face was to be seen. His repertoire included some clever verse, the best of it barbed with malice, the worst, sad doggerel.

Jimmy was born in 1841 in Carlisle. He tried to go to sea but is said to have 'blundered' his duties when thought to be an apprentice on HMS *Victory*. Back in Carlisle he began to play the fiddle, declaring himself to be 'a composer, vendor and singer of street ballads'. And so he was. The mining fraternity of West Cumberland especially liked him.

As the years passed his reputation grew and he styled himself the Cumberland Bard, and that is how many remember him. He died in 1903 in a workhouse in Carlisle and in modern times the city has put up a statue to his memory.

A pedlar calls on Mr and Mrs Tom Revell of the Swan Hotel, Newby Bridge. He was a familiar figure in Furness. A man not unlike him used to visit my grandparents annually. There would be a knock at the door and, on looking out, his trunk would already be open and the fairings on display. As my gran said: 'You felt you just had to buy something!'

When news travelled by handcart: Bob Carlisle keeps a firm hold on his Diorama travelling peep-show, seen in Carlisle after completing a walk, said to be of 5,419 miles (8,719km) to Lockerbie, before Christmas 1908. The Diorama included scenes from the Boer War, which Bob displayed by turning a handle. The pictures, lurid with bursting shells, showed British soldiers in South Africa advancing with fixed bayonets towards an unseen enemy. Another depicted the Relief of Ladysmith and the tears of joy of those liberated. Bob would visit Carlisle and tour nearby villages, where his show was a popular event. His naval cap and reefer jacket earned him the nickname of Captain Tugboat.

Opposite:

This bold lad standing in Fitz Park, Keswick, in 1906 is John William Dover, just back from Sheffield. At twelve years of age he sandpapered wooden bobbins in a Keswick bobbin mill. Later he joined his father, a stonemason, in Sheffield, though that work was not to last. As an old man living in Swarthmore, Ulverston, John remembered the day his father was dismissed …

I was in the sheds over at Sheffield shifting stone; my dad was a stonemason. I was about sixteen, then, and me dad he was dismissed. The boss wanted me to stay, begged and prayed for me ta stay. But I says no, where dad goes I go.

Dad could use a stone drill a treat. He could make windowsills, lovely sandstone, perfect chamfered. He got about sevenpence [3p] an hour; hod carriers got about fivepence an hour. I was a strong lad, and you needed ta be, lumping them loads all day. We earned well together, but we had to go.

We set off on the tramp home to Keswick. All t' way from Sheffield. Oh we seed a bit of the country. Took six months getting home. We got jobs. Come ta Yorkshire Bridge. Slept in barns and in t' night rats droppin' on you. We got into Manchester, slept in a lorry, a beer lorry, but nowt in it. We stopped at Chorley, a couple of months. It was good in Chorley. Aye, it was all reet. We got jobs helping build weaving sheds. Good bed every neet. You'd go ta bed certain hour every neet in a big model lodging house. Not a workhouse, see. Not that. About sixpence a neet.

Some old codgers there used ta wait of us coming from work every neet for drippings … off the teapots. I washed me shirt one day and put it to dry, and there was an old bugger who took it and put it on. But my old feller catched him and made him put it back. Oh, they were devils all right.

But we set off again for home, back to Cumberland, tramping to Preston and got a ha'porth of soup, a basin of soup for a halfpenny. Course I used to do a bit of asking, like, knocking at doors begging. In Lancaster just as I knocked at a door one woman said she'd seen a policeman and shoved me through the 'ouse out at the back.

The roads were a mess and me boots started comin' apart, flapping like. Well, we landed at Kendal and stayed in a lodging 'ouse. At Thirlmere we slept in a loft, then back to Keswick. I was about sixteen then. Aye, and proud. Proud of my dad. He was a good un was my dad.

A pony you might expect, or a horse, or even a donkey plodding up a Lakeland road pulling a cart, but an elephant is less than usual. Just one more of all those true stories that no one will believe when you arrive home after a night out with your pals.

Staff in hand, Owd Cooper, the Mallerstang postie, is off with the day's letters. Deliveries often meant a long trek to remote farms up in the fells. The strings, or *yorks*, round Owd Cooper's legs helped to keep his trousers from getting too wet. (It was drier once wellies came in.) My grandfather used to say that yorks stopped the rats running up inside your trousers, but my grandmother knew they were there to stop any money from dropping out.

Opposite:

One man forever travelling was John Jackson of Wateryeat, Blawith, seen with his cart as he delivers groceries to farms and cottages along the Coniston road in High Furness. John was one of many carriers who worked out of the towns of Ulverston, Keswick, Penrith and elsewhere, and regularly travelled the roads, collecting orders as they went. They delivered the goods, in some cases in the evening, but usually a week later.

The regular callers were varied and included the butcher, the fishmonger, the baker and the paraffin oil man. They arrived on their wagons or bikes, or sometimes just came pushing a handcart, travelling miles on their rounds.

By arrangement, a dressmaker would land with her sewing machine strapped to the pannier, to stay the week, living in at so much a day, plus her food, and doing repairs, but more usually making dresses from materials bought in town and already stored in the farmhouse cupboard.

Every now and then the sweep came, or a man on a bike with a gleaming pair of scissors, a sharpening stone and a cut-throat razor, prepared to give everyone (though generally only the men) from the master to the hired hands a good old haircut and neck scrape.

A powerful-looking dancing bear walks tall through Cockermouth. It's the 1890s and it was photographed in Main Street by W Youdale.

Performing bears toured the Cumbrian towns and villages, usually in the summer months, and were made to dance in the streets for a penny or two. There are numerous references to them dancing outside the Old England Hotel at Bowness, Windermere, as well as in Keswick, Kendal, and elsewhere.

The building behind the bear became the present Huntsman Inn, while the one to the right became the Appletree, and is now the Wordsworth Hotel where a bell near the arch was rung to call the crowds together at the Whitsun and Martinmas hirings.

A shaggy bear clings to a stick as it dances in a dusty Cumbrian road, believed to be at Oulton near Wigton. A tale exists that the bear arrived at a nearby inn, where the bear's keeper is supposed to have asked if they could sleep in a barn. A nervous landlord at first refused, but seeing that the creature was in a poor way, with its feet hot and bleeding, he relented and gave it water to drink and provided several more bucketfuls which were splashed on to its legs. Stories, of course, do tend to improve down the years.

Gypsy caravans on the road near Red Dial, Wigton.

Tanned faces, capable hands, a steady gaze — a gypsy couple stop for a bite and a drink in a disused roadside quarry near Greenodd, Ulverston.

Bibliography

Bradley, A G; *Highways and Byways in the Lake District*; London, 1903.

Bulmer, T (editor); *History, Topography and Directory of Furness and Cartmel*; 1910.

Carruthers, Frank J; *Lore of the Lake Country*; London, 1975.

Clare, T; *Archaeological Sites of the Lake District*; Derbyshire, 1981.

Collingwood, W G; *The Lake Counties*; London, 1932.

Crossland, J Brian; *Looking at Whitehaven*; Whitehaven, 1971.

Denyer, Susan; *Traditional Buildings and Life in the Lake District*; London, 1991.

Elder, Eleanor; *Travelling Players*; Plymouth, 1939.

Fraser, M; *Companion into Lakeland*; London, 1937.

Geddes, R Stanley; *Burlington Blue-Grey*; Barrow, 1975.

Geddling, Evelyn M; *Geddling's Dip*; Hexham, 1987.

Graham, Olivia; *Memoirs of a Lady Motorist*; London, 1916.

Griffin, A H; *A Lakeland Notebook*; London, 1975.

   Inside the Real Lakeland; Preston, 1970.

Hankinson, Alan; *The First Tigers*; London, 1972.

Hardy, Eric; *The Naturalist in Lakeland*; Newton Abbot, 1973.

Hart-Davis, Rupert; *Hugh Walpole*; London, 1952.

Hay, Daniel; *Whitehaven, A Short History*; Whitehaven, 1966.

Jenkinson, H I; *Jenkinson's Practical Guide to the English Lakes*; London, 1872.

Joy, David; *Railways of the Lake Counties*; Yorkshire, 1973.

Kemp, Laurie, and Templeton, Jim; *175 Years of Carlisle*; Runcorn, 1990.

Kirkby, B; *A Collection of Dialect Words and Phrases*; West Yorkshire, 1975.

Lancaster, J Y, and Wattleworth, D R; *The Iron and Steel Industry of West Cumberland*; Workington, 1977.

Lefebure, Molly; *Cumberland Heritage*; London, 1970.

Linder, Leslie; *The Journal of Beatrix Potter from 1881 to 1997*; London, 1966.

Mannix and Whellan; *History, Gazetteer and Directory of Cumberland 1947*.

Marshall, J D; *Old Lakeland, Some Cumbrian Social History*; Plymouth, 1971.

Marshall, J D, and Davies-Shiel, M; *The Lake District at Work*; Newton Abbot, 1971.

   Industrial Archaeology of the Lake Counties; Plymouth, 1969.

Nicholson, Norman; *Greater Lakeland*; London, 1969.

   The Lake District: An Anthology; London, 1977.

   The Lakers; Milnthorpe, 1955.

   Portrait of the Lakes; London, 1963.

   Wednesday Early Closing; London, 1975.

Pevsner, N; *Buildings of England: Cumberland and Westmorland*; London, 1967.

Postlethwaite, John; *Mines and Mining in the English Lake District*; Cumbria, 1975.

Ransome, Arthur; *The Autobiography of Arthur Ransome*; London, 1976.

Rawnsley, Eleanor F; *Canon Rawnsley, An Account of his Life*; Glasgow, 1923.

Rawnsley, H D; *Life and Nature at the English Lakes*; Glasgow, 1902.

Redmayne, W B; *Cumberland Scrapbook*; Carlisle, 1948.

Reed, David W; *Friends' School Wigton 1815-1953*; Carlisle, 1954.

Rice, H A L; *Lake Country Portraits*; London, 1967.

Rollinson, William; *A History of Cumberland and Westmorland*; London, 1978.

   A History of Man in the Lake District; London, 1967.

   The Lake District: Life and Traditions; London, 1996.

Scott, D; *Cumberland and Westmorland*; London, 1920.

Stockdale, J; *Annals of Cartmel*; Whitehaven, 1978.

Wainwright, A; *Pictorial Guides to the Lakeland Fells*; Kendal, 1955-1966.

Wyatt, John; *The Shining Levels*; London, 1973.

Index